Evolution

Second Edition

The Biozone Writing Team

Tracey Greenwood

Lissa Bainbridge-Smith

Kent Pryor

Richard Allan

Published by:
BIOZONE International Ltd
109 Cambridge Road, Hamilton 3216, New Zealand

Printed by REPLIKA PRESS PVT LTD using paper
produced from renewable and waste materials

Distribution Offices:

United Kingdom & Europe	**Biozone Learning Media (UK) Ltd**, UK
	Telephone: +44 1283-553-257
	Fax: +44 1283-553-258
	Email: sales@biozone.co.uk
	Website: www.biozone.co.uk
Australia	**Biozone Learning Media Australia**, Australia
	Telephone: +61 7-5535-4896
	Fax: +61 7-5508-2432
	Email: sales@biozone.com.au
	Website: www.biozone.com.au
USA, Canada, and ROW	**Biozone International Ltd**, New Zealand
	Telephone: +64 7-856 8104
	Fax: +64 7-856 9243
	Toll FREE phone: 1-866-556-2710 (USA-Canada only)
	Toll FREE fax: 1 800 717 8751 (USA-Canada only)
	Email: sales@biozone.co.nz
	Website: www.thebiozone.com

© 2012 **Biozone International Ltd**
ISBN: 978-1-877462-98-6
First edition 2006
Second edition 2012

Front cover photographs:
Fossil *Archaeopteryx*

Horseshoe crab (*Limulus polyphemus*) © iStock photos: ShaneKato photographer

Biology Modular Workbook Series

The BIOZONE *Biology Modular Workbook Series* has been developed to meet the demands of customers with the requirement for a flexible modular resource. Each workbook provides a collection of visually interesting and accessible activities, catering for students with a wide range of abilities and background. The workbooks are divided into a series of chapters, each comprising an introductory section and a series of write-on worksheets ranging from paper practicals and data handling exercises, to activities requiring critical thinking and analysis. Page tabs identifying "**Related activities**" and "**Weblinks**" help students to find related material within the workbook and locate online support that will enhance their understanding of the topic. During the development of this series, we have taken the opportunity to develop new content, while retaining the basic philosophy of a student-friendly resource, which spans the gulf between textbook and study guide. Its highly visual presentation engages students, increasing their motivation and empowering them to take control of their learning

Related Titles:

Skills in Biology

Evolution

This title in the *Biology Modular Workbook Series* provides students with a set of comprehensive guidelines and highly visual worksheets through which to explore aspects of population genetics and evolution. *Evolution* is the ideal companion for students of the life sciences. This workbook comprises five chapters, each of which covers a different aspect of evolutionary biology, explored through a series of concept-based activities. *Evolution* is a student-centered resource. Students completing the activities, in concert with their other classroom and practical work, will consolidate existing knowledge and develop and practise skills that they will use throughout their course. This workbook may be used in the classroom or at home as a supplement to a standard textbook. Some activities are introductory in nature, while others may be used to consolidate and test concepts already covered by other means. Biozone has a commitment to produce a cost-effective, high quality resource, which acts as a student's companion throughout their biology study. Please do not photocopy from this workbook; we cannot afford to provide single copies of workbooks to schools and continue to develop, update, and improve the material they contain.

Environmental Science

Acknowledgements and Photo Credits

Royalty free images, purchased by Biozone International Ltd, are used throughout this manual and have been obtained from the following sources: istockphotos (www.istockphoto.com) • Corel Corporation from various titles in their Professional Photos CD-ROM collection; ©Hemera Technologies Inc, 1997-2001; © 2005 JupiterImages Corporation www.clipart.com; PhotoDisc®, Inc. USA, www.photodisc.com.

Biozone's authors also acknowledge the generosity of those who have kindly provided information or photographs for this edition (some identified by way of coded credits): • Ben Lowe, University of Minnesota for advice and input on *Ensatina* subspecies and *Canis* distribution • Dept of Conservation for their invaluable assistance, especially Ferne McKenzie, for access to the DoC photo library • Sean Carroll and his text "*Endless forms most beautiful*" for authoritative information and examples for the new material on evolutionary developmental biology • Dr. Alan Cooper, Smithsonian Institute, for information on ratite evolution • The late Ron Lind, for photographs of stromatolites • Rita Willaert for the photograph of the Nuba woman • Aptychus for the photo of the Tamil girl • Dr. John Stencel for his data on the albino gray squirrel population • Andrew Dunn for his photo of the grove snail • Ewan Grant-Mackie and Prof. J.M. Grant-Mackie for information on the adaptive radiation of NZ wrens and the evolution of NZ parrots • Assoc. Prof. Bruce Clarkson, University of Waikato/CBER, for his contributions towards the activities on adaptive radiation in *Hebe* • Dept. of Natural Resources, Illinois, for information on genetic diversity in prairie chickens • Liam Nolan for his contributions to the activities on the genetic biodiversity of Antarctic springtails • Missouri Botanical Gardens for their photograph of egg mimicry in *Passiflora* • Alex Wild for his photograph of swollen thorn *Acacia* • California Academy of Sciences for the photograph of a Galápagos ground finch • Leo Sanchez and Burkhard Budel for use of their photographs used in the activities on Antarctic springtails • Chad Lane for the photo of the yellow-eyed *Ensatina* • Walter Siegmund for the photo of the checkerspot butterfly

We also acknowledge the photographers that have made their images available through Wikimedia Commons under Creative Commons Licences 2.0, 2.5. or 3.0 (as identified in the text): • D. Gordon E. Robertson • J.M.Garg • Omasz G. Sienicki • Laitche • Utahcamera • Aviceda • Allan and Elaine Wilson • Bruce Marlin • Lorax • Onno Zweers • AKA • Dirk Beyer • Veleda • Jim Gifford

Coded credits as follows: **CDC**: Centers for Disease Control and Prevention **DoC**: Department of Conservation (NZ), **DoC-CV**: C.R. Veitch, **RM-DoC**: Rod Morris, **EII**: Education Interactive Imaging, **NASA**: National Aeronautics and Space Administration, **RA**: Richard Allan, **RCN**: Ralph Cocklin, **USDA**: US Department of Agriculture

Genes & Inheritance

Human Evolution

Contents

CODES: Δ **Upgraded** this edition ☆ **New** this edition   **Activity** is marked: ☐ to be done; ☑ when completed

How to Use this Workbook

Evolution is designed to provide students with a resource that will make it easier to acquire skills and knowledge in this exciting field of study. An appreciation of the overwhelming evidence for evolution and an understanding of evolutionary mechanisms are central to most biology curricula. Evidence provided by new gene technologies is increasingly adding to our current understanding of how and why populations change and such knowledge is increasingly relevant in today's rapidly changing world. This workbook is suitable for all students of the life sciences, and will reinforce and extend the ideas developed by teachers. It is **not a textbook**; its aim is to complement the texts written for your particular course. *Evolution* provides the following resources. in each chapter. You should refer back to them as you work through each set of worksheets.

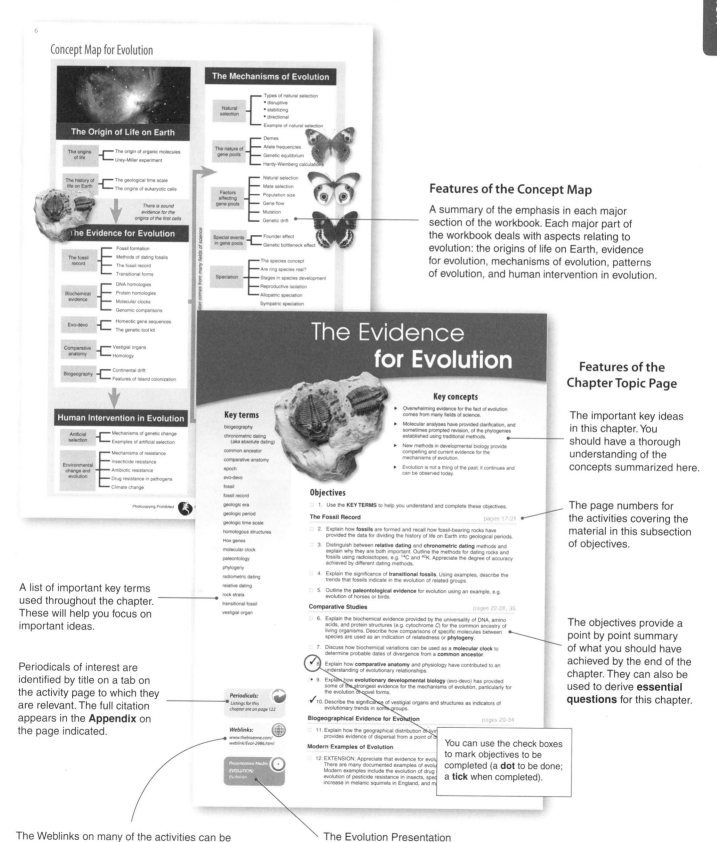

Features of the Concept Map

A summary of the emphasis in each major section of the workbook. Each major part of the workbook deals with aspects relating to evolution: the origins of life on Earth, evidence for evolution, mechanisms of evolution, patterns of evolution, and human intervention in evolution.

Features of the Chapter Topic Page

The important key ideas in this chapter. You should have a thorough understanding of the concepts summarized here.

The page numbers for the activities covering the material in this subsection of objectives.

The objectives provide a point by point summary of what you should have achieved by the end of the chapter. They can also be used to derive **essential questions** for this chapter.

A list of important key terms used throughout the chapter. These will help you focus on important ideas.

Periodicals of interest are identified by title on a tab on the activity page to which they are relevant. The full citation appears in the **Appendix** on the page indicated.

You can use the check boxes to mark objectives to be completed (a **dot** to be done; a **tick** when completed).

The Weblinks on many of the activities can be accessed through the web links page at: *www.thebiozone.com/weblink/Evol-2986.html* See page 3 for more details.

The Evolution Presentation Media covers the material listed under this heading.

Using the Activities

The activities and exercises make up most of the content of this workbook. They are designed to reinforce concepts in the topic. Your teacher may use the activity pages to introduce a topic for the first time, or you may use them to revise ideas already covered. They are excellent for use in the classroom, and as homework exercises and revision. In most cases, the activities should not be attempted until you have carried out the necessary background reading from your textbook.

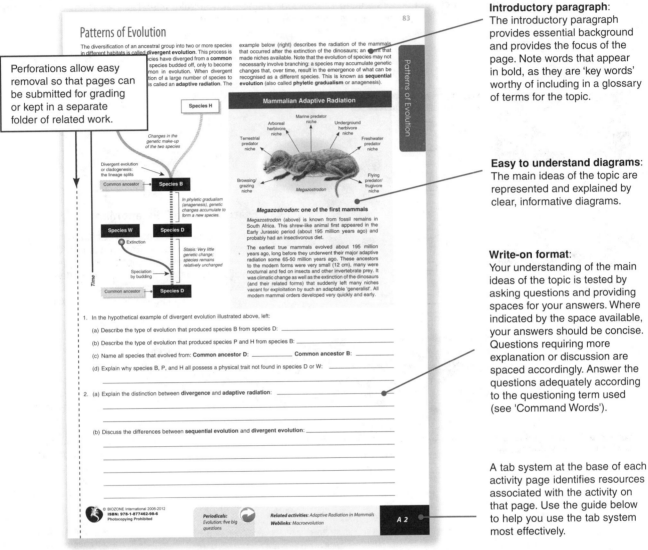

Perforations allow easy removal so that pages can be submitted for grading or kept in a separate folder of related work.

Introductory paragraph:
The introductory paragraph provides essential background and provides the focus of the page. Note words that appear in bold, as they are 'key words' worthy of including in a glossary of terms for the topic.

Easy to understand diagrams:
The main ideas of the topic are represented and explained by clear, informative diagrams.

Write-on format:
Your understanding of the main ideas of the topic is tested by asking questions and providing spaces for your answers. Where indicated by the space available, your answers should be concise. Questions requiring more explanation or discussion are spaced accordingly. Answer the questions adequately according to the questioning term used (see 'Command Words').

A tab system at the base of each activity page identifies resources associated with the activity on that page. Use the guide below to help you use the tab system most effectively.

Using page tabs more effectively

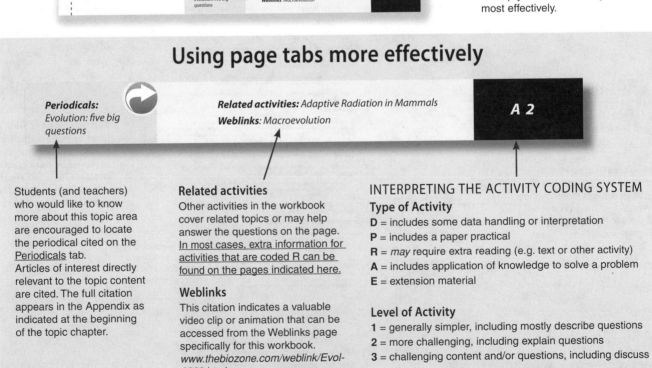

Periodicals:
Evolution: five big questions

Related activities: Adaptive Radiation in Mammals
Weblinks: Macroevolution

A 2

Students (and teachers) who would like to know more about this topic area are encouraged to locate the periodical cited on the Periodicals tab.
Articles of interest directly relevant to the topic content are cited. The full citation appears in the Appendix as indicated at the beginning of the topic chapter.

Related activities
Other activities in the workbook cover related topics or may help answer the questions on the page. In most cases, extra information for activities that are coded R can be found on the pages indicated here.

Weblinks
This citation indicates a valuable video clip or animation that can be accessed from the Weblinks page specifically for this workbook.
www.thebiozone.com/weblink/Evol-2986.html

INTERPRETING THE ACTIVITY CODING SYSTEM

Type of Activity
D = includes some data handling or interpretation
P = includes a paper practical
R = may require extra reading (e.g. text or other activity)
A = includes application of knowledge to solve a problem
E = extension material

Level of Activity
1 = generally simpler, including mostly describe questions
2 = more challenging, including explain questions
3 = challenging content and/or questions, including discuss

Using BIOZONE's Website

The current internet address (URL) for the web site is displayed here. You can type a new address directly into this space.

Use Google to search for web sites of interest. The more precise your search words are, the better the list of results. EXAMPLE: If you type in "biotechnology", your search will return an overwhelmingly large number of sites, many of which will not be useful to you. Be more specific, e.g. "biotechnology medicine DNA uses".

Find out about our superb **Presentation Media**. These slide shows are designed to provide in-depth, highly accessible illustrative material and notes on specific areas of biology.

News: Find out about product announcements, shipping dates, and workshops and trade displays by Biozone at teachers' conferences around the world.

Access the **Biolnks** database of web sites related to each major area of biology. It's a great way to quickly find out more on topics of interest.

Weblinks: www.thebiozone.com/weblink/Evol-2986.html

BOOKMARK WEBLINKS BY TYPING IN THE ADDRESS: IT IS NOT ACCESSIBLE DIRECTLY FROM BIOZONE'S WEBSITE

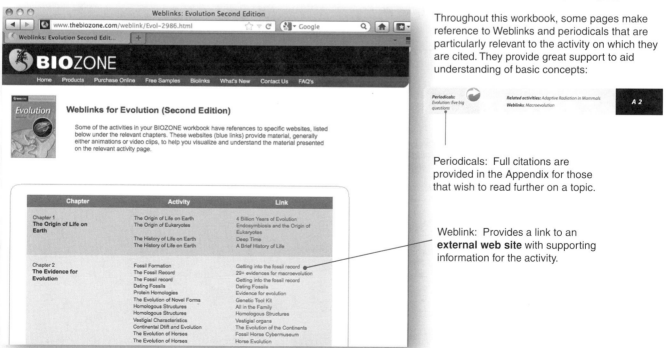

Throughout this workbook, some pages make reference to Weblinks and periodicals that are particularly relevant to the activity on which they are cited. They provide great support to aid understanding of basic concepts:

Periodicals: Full citations are provided in the Appendix for those that wish to read further on a topic.

Weblink: Provides a link to an **external web site** with supporting information for the activity.

4

Resources Information

Your set textbook should always be a starting point for information, but there are also many other resources available. A list of readily available resources is provided below. Access to the publishers of these resources can be made directly from Biozone's web site. Please note that our listing of any product in this workbook does not denote Biozone's endorsement of it.

Supplementary Texts

Carroll, S.B., 2008.
Into the Jungle: Great Adventures in the Search for Evolution, 224 pp.
Publisher: Benjamin Cummings
ISBN: 0-3215-5671-2
Comments: *Nine stories documenting some of the discoveries that have shaped our understanding of evolution. This collection targets those learning the basics of evolutionary biology.*

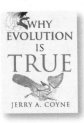

Coyne, J.A., 2009.
Why Evolution is True, 304 pp.
Publisher: Viking Adult
ISBN: 0-6700-2053-2
Comments: *An up-to-date volume summarizing recent evidence in support of evolution from the fields of genetics, paleontology, geology, molecular biology, and anatomy. It provides a concise, easy to read overview.*

Futuyma, D.J., 2009
Evolution, 545 p
Publisher: Sinauer Associates
ISBN: 0-8789-3223-2
Comments: *'Evolution' addresses the history of evolution, evolutionary processes, and the nature of adaptation within a framework spanning all levels of biological organization.*

Lane, N., 2010.
Life Ascending: The Ten Great Inventions of Evolution 352 pp.
ISBN: 0-3930-6596-0
Publisher: W. W. Norton & Company
Comments: *This very interesting book describes the ten greatest "biological inventions" of evolution (e.g. origin of life, DNA, photosynthesis, and vision).*

Martin, R.A., 2004.
Missing Links, 302 pp.
ISBN: 0-7637-2196-4
This book introduces evolutionary science with an accessible discussion of basic scientific practices, rock and fossil dating techniques, and schools of classification. Examples of evolutionary transition are provided, from the origins of life to the morphological changes that readers will observe in their lifetimes.

Palmer, D., 2009.
Evolution The Story of Life, 374 pp.
ISBN: 9780520255111
Publisher: University of California Press
Comments: *This highly visual book documents the 3.5 billion year journey of life and evolution on Earth. It takes a strictly cladistic view so may feel unfamiliar to those used to traditional classification schemes.*

Weiner, J., 1994.
The Beak of the Finch: A Story of Evolution in Our Time, 332 pp.
Publisher: Knopf
ISBN: 0-6794-0003-6
Jonathan Weiner details the work of two scientists, Peter and Rosemary Grant, as they document the evolution of Darwin's finches on the Galápagos Islands.

Zimmer, C., 2001
Evolution: The Triumph of an Idea, 362 pp. (hardback)
Publisher: HarperCollins
ISBN: 0-06-019906-7
Comments: *A vivid, accessible exploration of Darwin's ideas; essential for those who wish to explore the origin and diversification of life.*

Periodicals, Magazines, & Journals

Biological Sciences Review: *An informative quarterly publication for biology students.* Enquiries: **UK**: Philip Allan Publishers **Tel**: 01869 338652 **Fax**: 01869 338803 **E-mail**: sales@philipallan.co.uk **Australasia**: **Tel**: 08 8278 5916, **E-mail**: rjmorton@adelaide.on.net

New Scientist: *Widely available weekly magazine with research summaries and features.* Enquiries: Reed Business Information Ltd, 51 Wardour St. London WIV 4BN **Tel**: (UK and intl):+44 (0) 1444 475636 **E-mail**: ns.subs@qss-uk.com *or subscribe from their web site.*

Scientific American: *A monthly magazine containing specialist features. Articles range in level of reading difficulty and assumed knowledge.* Subscription enquiries: 415 Madison Ave. New York. NY10017-1111 **Tel**: (outside North America): 515-247-7631 **Tel**: (US& Canada): 800-333-1199

School Science Review: *A quarterly journal which includes articles, reviews, and news on current research and curriculum development. Free to Ordinary Members of the ASE or available on subscription.* Enquiries: **Tel**: 01707 28300 **Email**: info@ase.org.uk *or visit their web site.*

The American Biology Teacher: *The peer-reviewed journal of the NABT. Published nine times a year and containing information and activities relevant to biology teachers.* Contact: NABT, 12030 Sunrise Valley Drive, #110, Reston, VA 20191-3409 **Web**: www.nabt.org

Command Words

Questions come in a variety of forms. Whether you are studying for an exam or writing an essay, it is important to understand exactly what the question is asking. A question has two parts to it: one part of the question will provide you with information, the second part of the question will provide you with instructions as to how to answer the question. Following these instructions is most important. Often students in examinations know the material but fail to follow instructions and do not answer the question appropriately. Examiners often use certain key words to introduce questions. Look out for them and be clear as to what they mean. Below is a description of terms commonly used when asking questions in biology.

Commonly used Terms in Biology

The following terms are frequently used when asking questions in examinations and assessments. Students should have a clear understanding of each of the following terms and use this understanding to answer questions appropriately.

Account for: Provide a satisfactory explanation or reason for an observation.

Analyze: Interpret data to reach stated conclusions.

Annotate: Add **brief** notes to a diagram, drawing or graph.

Apply: Use an idea, equation, principle, theory, or law in a new situation.

Appreciate: To understand the meaning or relevance of a particular situation.

Calculate: Find an answer using mathematical methods. Show the working unless instructed not to.

Compare: Give an account of similarities and differences between two or more items, referring to both (or all) of them throughout. Comparisons can be given using a table. Comparisons generally ask for similarities more than differences (see contrast).

Construct: Represent or develop in graphical form.

Contrast: Show differences. Set in opposition.

Deduce: Reach a conclusion from information given.

Define: Give the precise meaning of a word or phrase as concisely as possible.

Derive: Manipulate a mathematical equation to give a new equation or result.

Describe: Give an account, including all the relevant information.

Design: Produce a plan, object, simulation or model.

Determine: Find the only possible answer.

Discuss: Give an account including, where possible, a range of arguments, assessments of the relative importance of various factors, or comparison of alternative hypotheses.

Distinguish: Give the difference(s) between two or more different items.

Draw: Represent by means of pencil lines. Add labels unless told not to do so.

Estimate: Find an approximate value for an unknown quantity, based on the information provided and application of scientific knowledge.

Evaluate: Assess the implications and limitations.

Explain: Give a clear account including causes, reasons, or mechanisms.

Identify: Find an answer from a number of possibilities.

Illustrate: Give concrete examples. Explain clearly by using comparisons or examples.

Interpret: Comment upon, give examples, describe relationships. Describe, then evaluate.

List: Give a sequence of names or other brief answers with no elaboration. Each one should be clearly distinguishable from the others.

Measure: Find a value for a quantity.

Outline: Give a brief account or summary. Include essential information only.

Predict: Give an expected result.

Solve: Obtain an answer using algebraic and/or numerical methods.

State: Give a specific name, value, or other answer. No supporting argument or calculation is necessary.

Suggest: Propose a hypothesis or other possible explanation.

Summarize: Give a brief, condensed account. Include conclusions and avoid unnecessary details.

In Conclusion

Students should familiarize themselves with this list of terms and, where necessary throughout the course, they should refer back to them when answering questions. The list of terms mentioned above is not exhaustive and students should compare this list with past examination papers and essays etc. and add any new terms (and their meaning) to the list above. The aim is to become familiar with interpreting the question and answering it appropriately.

Concept Map for Evolution

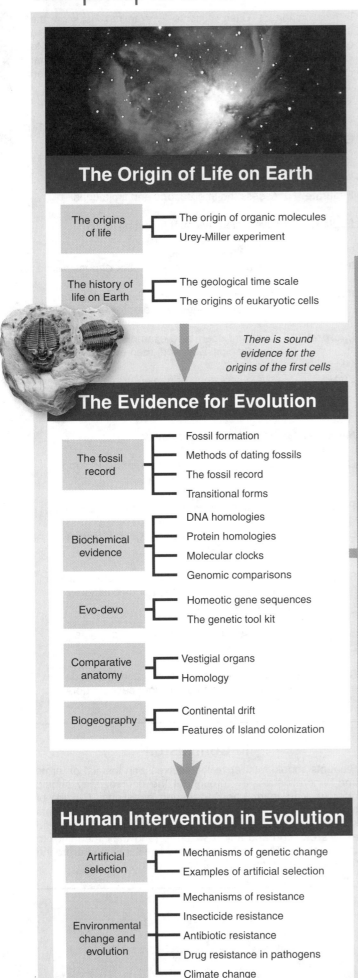
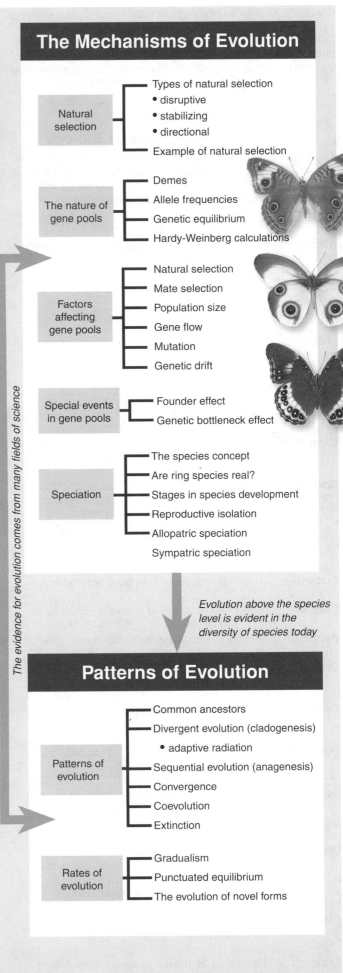

The Origin of Life on Earth

The origins of life
- The origin of organic molecules
- Urey-Miller experiment

The history of life on Earth
- The geological time scale
- The origins of eukaryotic cells

There is sound evidence for the origins of the first cells

The Evidence for Evolution

The fossil record
- Fossil formation
- Methods of dating fossils
- The fossil record
- Transitional forms

Biochemical evidence
- DNA homologies
- Protein homologies
- Molecular clocks
- Genomic comparisons

Evo-devo
- Homeotic gene sequences
- The genetic tool kit

Comparative anatomy
- Vestigial organs
- Homology

Biogeography
- Continental drift
- Features of Island colonization

Human Intervention in Evolution

Artificial selection
- Mechanisms of genetic change
- Examples of artificial selection

Environmental change and evolution
- Mechanisms of resistance
- Insecticide resistance
- Antibiotic resistance
- Drug resistance in pathogens
- Climate change

The evidence for evolution comes from many fields of science

The Mechanisms of Evolution

Natural selection
- Types of natural selection
  - disruptive
  - stabilizing
  - directional
- Example of natural selection

The nature of gene pools
- Demes
- Allele frequencies
- Genetic equilibrium
- Hardy-Weinberg calculations

Factors affecting gene pools
- Natural selection
- Mate selection
- Population size
- Gene flow
- Mutation
- Genetic drift

Special events in gene pools
- Founder effect
- Genetic bottleneck effect

Speciation
- The species concept
- Are ring species real?
- Stages in species development
- Reproductive isolation
- Allopatric speciation
- Sympatric speciation

Evolution above the species level is evident in the diversity of species today

Patterns of Evolution

Patterns of evolution
- Common ancestors
- Divergent evolution (cladogenesis)
  - adaptive radiation
- Sequential evolution (anagenesis)
- Convergence
- Coevolution
- Extinction

Rates of evolution
- Gradualism
- Punctuated equilibrium
- The evolution of novel forms

   © BIOZONE International 2006-2012

The Origin of Life on Earth

Key terms

Archaea
Bacteria (=Eubacteria)
chronometric dating
endosymbiosis
endosymbiotic theory
eon
epoch
era
Eukarya
fossil
fossil record
geologic time scale
Miller-Urey experiments
panspermia
period
primordial environment
radiometric dating
relative dating
rock strata
transitional fossil

Key concepts

▶ The primordial environment on Earth was important in the origin of the first organic compounds.

▶ Fossilized cyanobacterial colonies provide evidence of life 3.5 billion years ago.

▶ The dating of the fossil record gives a history of life on Earth and a geologic time scale.

▶ The endosymbiotic theory provides a working model for the origin of eukaryotes.

Objectives

☐ 1. Use the **KEY TERMS** to help you understand and complete these objectives.

The Origin of Life on Earth pages 8-12

☐ 2. Describe the **primordial environment** and the likely events that led to the formation of life on Earth.

☐ 3. Recognize major stages in the evolution of life on Earth. Summarize the main ideas related to where life originated: ocean surface, extraterrestrial (**panspermia**), and deep sea thermal vents.

☐ 4. Outline the experiments of **Miller** and **Urey** that attempted to simulate the prebiotic environment on Earth. Describe their importance in our understanding of the probable origin of organic compounds.

☐ 5. Describe the likely role of RNA as the first self-replicating molecule. Outline its role as an enzyme and in the origin of the first self-replicating cells.

☐ 6. Describe the evidence for the first aquatic prokaryotes. Discuss the importance of these early organisms to the later evolution of diversity.

☐ 7. Explain what the current ecology of some bacterial groups (Bacteria and Archaea) tells us about the probable conditions of early life on Earth.

☐ 8. Discuss the possible origin of membranes and the first prokaryotic cells.

☐ 9. Discuss the **endosymbiotic** (endosymbiont) theory for the evolution of eukaryotic cells. Summarize the evidence in support of this theory.

The History of Life on Earth pages 13-14

☐ 10. Explain how the dating of fossil-bearing rocks has provided the data for dividing the history of life on Earth into geological periods, which collectively form the **geologic time scale**. Explain how spans of time on the geologic time scale are marked by major geological or paleontological events, such as mass extinctions.

☐ 11. Distinguish **eons** from **eras** and recognize the broad characteristics of each of the eras in the geological time scale since ~600 million years ago (including climate changes and episodes of mountain building).

Periodicals:
Listings for this chapter are on page 122

Weblinks:
*www.thebiozone.com/
weblink/Evol-2986.html*

*Presentation Media
EVOLUTION:
The Origin of Life*

Life in the Universe

Life 'as we know it' requires three basic ingredients: a source of energy, carbon, and liquid water. Complex organic molecules (as are found in living things) have been detected beyond Earth in interstellar dust clouds and in meteorites that have landed on Earth. More than 4 billion years ago, one such dust cloud collapsed into a swirling **accretion disk** that gave rise to the sun and planets. Some of the fragile molecules survived the heat of solar system formation by sticking together in comets at the disk's fringe where temperatures were freezing. Later, the comets and other cloud remnants carried the molecules to Earth.

The formation of these organic molecules and their significance to the origin of life on Earth are currently being investigated experimentally (see below). The study of the origin of life on Earth is closely linked to the search for life elsewhere in our solar system. There are further plans to send solar and lunar orbiters to other planets and their moons, and even to land on a comet in November 2014. Their objective will be to look for signs of life (present or past) or its chemical precursors. If detected, such a discovery would suggest that life (at least 'primitive' life) may be widespread in the universe.

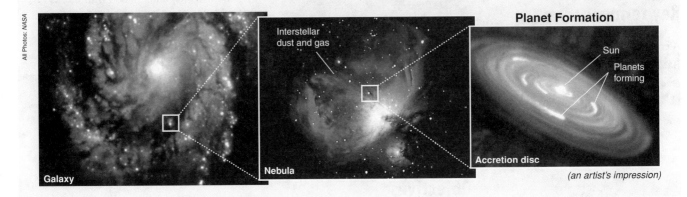

Galaxy

Interstellar dust and gas

Nebula

Planet Formation

Sun

Planets forming

Accretion disc

(an artist's impression)

How Organic Molecules Might Form in Space

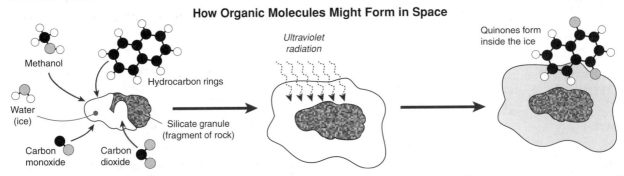

Methanol

Hydrocarbon rings

Water (ice)

Carbon monoxide

Carbon dioxide

Silicate granule (fragment of rock)

Ultraviolet radiation

Quinones form inside the ice

Interstellar ice begins to form when molecules such as methanol, water, and hydrocarbon freeze onto sandlike granules of silicate drifting in dense interstellar clouds.

Ultraviolet radiation from nearby stars cause some of the chemical bonds of the frozen compounds in the ice to break.

The broken down molecules recombine into structures such as quinones, which would never form if the fragments were free to float away.

Two **Mars Exploration rovers** landed on Mars in early 2004. Each rover carried sophisticated instruments, which were used to determine the history of climate and water at two sites where conditions may once have been favourable for life.

Organic Molecules Detected in Space

In a simple cloud-chamber experiment with simulated space ice (frozen water, methanol, and ammonia), complex compounds were yielded, including: ketones, nitriles, ethers, alcohols, and quinones (nearly identical in structure to those that help chlorophyll). These same organic molecules are found in carbon-rich meteorites. A six-carbon molecule (known as HMT) was also created. In warm, acidic water it is known to produce amino acids.

In another investigation into compounds produced in this way, some of the molecules displayed a tendency to form capsule-like droplets in water. These capsules were similar to those produced using extracts of a meteorite from Murchison, Australia in 1989. When organic compounds from the meteorite were mixed with water, they spontaneously assembled into spherical structures similar to cell membranes. These capsules were found to be made up of a host of complex organic molecules.

Source: *Life's far-flung raw materials*, Scientific American, July 1999, pp. 26-33

1. Suggest how sampling the chemical makeup of a comet might assist our understanding of life's origins:

   _____

2. Explain the significance of molecules from space that naturally form capsule-like droplets when added to water:

   _____

3. Explain how scientists are able to know about the existence of complex organic molecules in space: _____

   _____

Related activities: The Origin of Life on Earth

Periodicals: The ice of life, Life's far flung raw materials

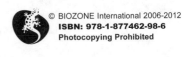

© BIOZONE International 2006-2012
ISBN: 978-1-877462-98-6
Photocopying Prohibited

The Origin of Life on Earth

Recent discoveries of **prebiotic** conditions on other planets and their moons has rekindled interest in the origin of life on primeval Earth. Experiments demonstrate that both peptides and nucleic acids may form polymers naturally in the conditions that are thought to have existed in a primitive terrestrial environment. RNA has also been shown to have enzymatic properties (**ribozymes**) and is capable of self-replication. These discoveries have removed some fundamental obstacles to creating a plausible scientific model for the origin of life from a prebiotic soup. Much research is now underway and space probes have been sent to Mercury, Venus, Mars, Pluto and its moon, Charon. They will search for evidence of prebiotic conditions or primitive microorganisms. The study of life in such regions beyond our planet is called **exobiology**.

Steps Proposed in the Origin of Life

The appearance of life on our planet may be understood as the result of evolutionary processes involving the following major steps:

1. Formation of the Earth (4600 mya) and its acquisition of volatile organic chemicals by collision with comets and meteorites, which provided the precursors of biochemical molecules.

2. Prebiotic synthesis and accumulation of amino acids, purines, pyrimidines, sugars, lipids, and other organic molecules in the primitive terrestrial environment.

3. Prebiotic condensation reactions involving the synthesis of polymers of peptides (proteins), and nucleic acids (most probably just RNA) with self-replicating and catalytic (enzymatic) abilities.

4. Synthesis of lipids, their self-assembly into double-layered membranes and liposomes, and the 'capturing' of prebiotic (self-replicating and catalytic) molecules within their boundaries.

5. Formation of a **protobiont**; this is an immediate precursor to the first living systems. Such protobionts would exhibit cooperative interactions between small catalytic peptides, replicative molecules, proto-tRNA, and protoribosomes.

An RNA World

RNA is able to act as a vehicle for both information storage and catalysis. It therefore provides a way around the problem that genes require enzymes to form and enzymes require genes to form. The first stage of evolution may have proceeded by RNA molecules performing the catalytic activities necessary to assemble themselves from a nucleotide soup. RNA molecules could then begin to synthesize proteins. There is a problem with RNA as a prebiotic molecule because the ribose is unstable. This has led to the idea of a pre-RNA world (PNA).

Photo: Ron Lind

These living **stromatolites** from a beach in Western Australia are created by mats of cyanobacteria. Similar, fossilized sy have been found in rocks dating back to 3500 million years ago.

Dynamics of an RNA World

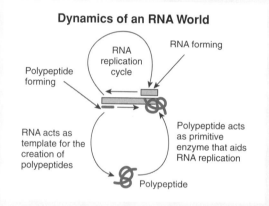

RNA replication cycle

RNA forming

Polypeptide forming

RNA acts as template for the creation of polypeptides

Polypeptide acts as primitive enzyme that aids RNA replication

Polypeptide

Scenarios for the Origin of Life

The origin of life remains a matter of scientific speculation. Three alternative views of how the key processes occurred are illustrated below:

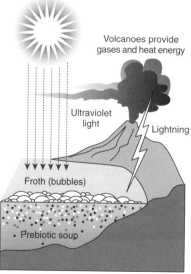

Volcanoes provide gases and heat energy

Ultraviolet light

Lightning

Froth (bubbles)

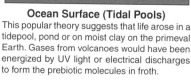

Prebiotic soup

Ocean Surface (Tidal Pools)

This popular theory suggests that life arose in a tidepool, pond or on moist clay on the primeval Earth. Gases from volcanoes would have been energized by UV light or electrical discharges to form the prebiotic molecules in froth.

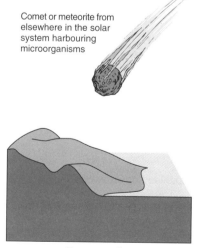

Comet or meteorite from elsewhere in the solar system harbouring microorganisms

Panspermia

Cosmic ancestry (panspermia) is a serious scientific theory that proposes living organisms were 'seeded' on Earth as 'passengers' aboard comets or meteors. Such incoming organisms would have to survive the heat of re-entry.

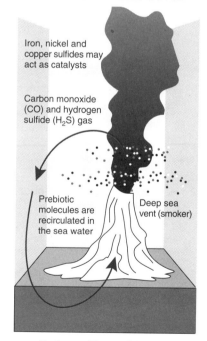

Iron, nickel and copper sulfides may act as catalysts

Carbon monoxide (CO) and hydrogen sulfide (H_2S) gas

Prebiotic molecules are recirculated in the sea water

Deep sea vent (smoker)

Undersea Thermal Vents

A recently proposed theory suggests that life may have arisen at ancient volcanic vents (called smokers). This environment provides the necessary gases, energy, and a possible source of catalysts (metal sulfides).

© BIOZONE International 2006-2011
ISBN: 978-1-877462-98-6
Photocopying Prohibited

Periodicals:
A simpler origin of life, Primeval pools

Related activities: Prebiotic Experiments
Weblinks: 4 Billion Years of Evolution

A 2

Landmarks in the Origin and Evolution of Life

Geological column

Today —

1.0 —

Billions of years ago (bya)

2.0 —

3.0 —

4.0 —

4.6 —

Fossil history of large eukaryotic organisms is well documented.

0.55 bya: Fossils of more complex, multicelled creatures were thought to have first appeared here (but see below). Fossils 600-540 my old, reaching 1 metre across have been found in the Ediacara Hills, Flinders Ranges, South Australia.

1.1 bya: Grooves in sandstone from the Vindhyan Basin, central India, may be the burrows of ancient worm-like creatures. This is 500 million years earlier than any previous evidence for multicellular animals.

2.1 bya: First fossil imprints appear in the geological record that are so large they can only be eukaryotes.

2.5 bya: Molecular fossil of cyanobacteria, 2-methylhopane, is abundant in organic-rich sedimentary rocks from the Mount McRae shale in Western Australia.

2.7 bya: Compounds in the oily residue squeezed out of Australian shale suggest the presence of eukaryotic cells. It appears to push the beginnings of complex life on Earth a billion years earlier than scientists had first thought.

3.5 bya: The oldest microbial community now known is from the Apex chert of northwestern Western Australia. It is a diverse assemblage of cyanobacteria fossils, leaving behind big, layered mounds of fossil bacterial colonies (stromatolites).

A series of prebiotic steps that lead to the formation of the **protobiont**; an immediate precursor to the first living systems.

4.6 bya: Formation of the Earth and its acquisition of volatile organic chemicals by collision with comets and meteorites, which provided the precursors of biochemical molecules.

A black smoker: In 1977, a vent was discovered at the Galapagos spreading center (mid-oceanic ridge), out of which gushed hot water laden with dissolved minerals. Since this discovery, hydrothermal venting has been found to be common along the length of the 55,000 km ridge crest system. Such black smokers are named after the dirty looking, high temperature water (350°C) that gushes from the chimney structures that they form. Such an environment is thought to be a possible site for prebiotic synthesis of life's molecules.

1. Summarize the three most accepted scientific models for the origin of life on Earth:

   (a) Ocean surface: _____

   _____

   _____

   (b) Panspermia: _____

   _____

   _____

   (c) Undersea thermal vents: _____

   _____

   _____

2. How did the discovery of ribozymes assist in creating a plausible model for the prebiotic origin of life?

   _____

   _____

3. How old are the earliest fossils of microscopic life known to be? _____

4. Scientists are seriously looking for evidence of life on other planets of our solar system, as well as some of their moons.

   (a) Name a planet or a moon that is a pending target for such spacecraft missions: _____

   (b) How might the discovery of life elsewhere in our solar system influence probable explanations for the origin of life?

   _____

   _____

© BIOZONE International 2006-2012
ISBN: 978-1-877462-98-6
Photocopying Prohibited

KEY TERMS: Crossword

Complete the crossword below, which will test your understanding of key terms in this chapter and their meanings.

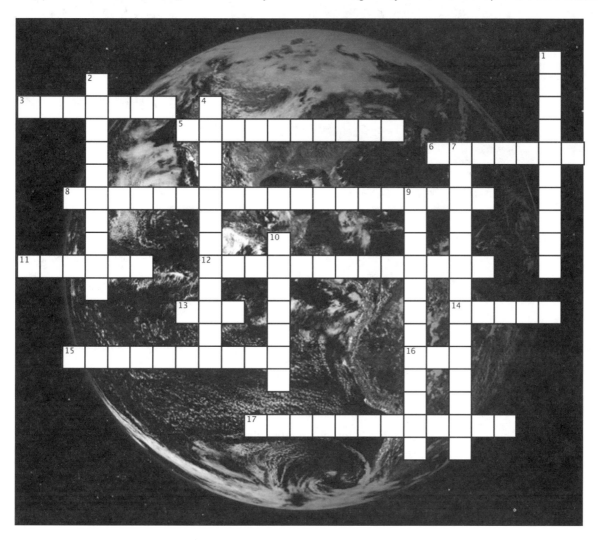

Clues Across

3. A domain of all the eukaryotic organisms on Earth.
5. Layers of rock or soil with distinguishing characteristics. (2 words; 4, 6)
6. An ancient bacterial group that occupies extreme environments on Earth today.
8. A system of chronological measurement relating stratigraphy to time. (3 words; 10, 4, 5)
11. A division of the geologic timescale that subdivides eras, and are themselves subdivided into epochs.
12. The term used to describe the theory of evolution of eukaryotic cells from large prokaryotic cells.
13. The longest division of geologic time, containing two or more eras.
14. The name of a subdivision of a period, that is then subdivided into ages.
15. Name given to the rich chemical environment in which the first cells arose some 3500 million years ago.
16. The name of a main division of the geological timescale, that is subdivided into periods.
17. Name given to a type of fossil that illustrates an evolutionary transition. They possess both primitive and derived characteristics.

Clues Down

1. The name of an experiment that simulated hypothetical conditions thought at the time to be present on primitive Earth. (2 words; 6, 4)
2. The theory that proposes that living organisms were seeded on Earth from extraterrestrial material.
4. The sum total of current paleontological knowledge. (2 words; 6, 6)
7. A dating method used to determine the relative order of past events, without necessarily determining their absolute age. (2 words; 8, 6)
9. This type of rock and fossil dating determines absolute age and is often based on radioisotopic methods
10. The remains of long-dead organisms that have escaped decay and have become part of the Earth's crust.

The Evidence for Evolution

Key concepts

► Overwhelming evidence for the fact of evolution comes from many fields of science.

► Molecular analyses have provided clarification, and sometimes prompted revision, of the phylogenies established using traditional methods.

► New methods in developmental biology provide compelling and current evidence for the mechanisms of evolution.

► Evolution is not a thing of the past; it continues and can be observed today.

Key terms

biogeography

chronometric dating
(*aka* absolute dating)

common ancestor

comparative anatomy

epoch

evo-devo

fossil

fossil record

geologic era

geologic period

geologic time scale

homologous structures

Hox genes

molecular clock

paleontology

phylogeny

radiometric dating

relative dating

rock strata

transitional fossil

vestigial organ

Objectives

☐ 1. Use the **KEY TERMS** to help you understand and complete these objectives.

The Fossil Record   pages 17-21

☐ 2. Explain how **fossils** are formed and recall how fossil-bearing rocks have provided the data for dividing the history of life on Earth into geological periods.

☐ 3. Distinguish between **relative dating** and **chronometric dating** methods and explain why they are both important. Outline the methods for dating rocks and fossils using radioisotopes, e.g. ^{14}C and ^{40}K. Appreciate the degree of accuracy achieved by different dating methods.

☐ 4. Explain the significance of **transitional fossils**. Using examples, describe the trends that fossils indicate in the evolution of related groups.

☐ 5. Outline the **paleontological evidence** for evolution using an example, e.g. evolution of horses or birds.

Comparative Studies   pages 22-28, 35

☐ 6. Explain the biochemical evidence provided by the universality of DNA, amino acids, and protein structures (e.g. cytochrome *C*) for the common ancestry of living organisms. Describe how comparisons of specific molecules between species are used as an indication of relatedness or **phylogeny**.

☐ 7. Discuss how biochemical variations can be used as a **molecular clock** to determine probable dates of divergence from a **common ancestor**.

☐ 8. Explain how **comparative anatomy** and physiology have contributed to an understanding of evolutionary relationships.

☐ 9. Explain how **evolutionary developmental biology** (evo-devo) has provided some of the strongest evidence for the mechanisms of evolution, particularly for the evolution of novel forms.

☐ 10. Describe the significance of vestigial organs and structures as indicators of evolutionary trends in some groups.

Biogeographical Evidence for Evolution   pages 29-34

☐ 11. Explain how the geographical distribution of living and extinct organisms provides evidence of dispersal from a point of origin across pre-existing barriers.

Modern Examples of Evolution   pages 45-52, 113-118

☐ 12. EXTENSION: Appreciate that evidence for evolution is not confined to the past. There are many documented examples of evolution occurring in the present day. Modern examples include the evolution of drug resistance in pathogens, the evolution of pesticide resistance in insects, speciation in Hawaiian *Drosophila*, increase in melanic squirrels in England, and many others.

Periodicals:
Listings for this chapter are on page 122

Weblinks:
www.thebiozone.com/
weblink/Evol-2986.html

Presentation Media
EVOLUTION:
Evolution

The Fossil Record

Relative dating establishes the sequential (relative) order of past events in a rock profile, but it can not provide an absolute date for an event. Each rock layer (strata) is unique in terms of the type of rock (sedimentary or volcanic) and the type of fossils it contains. Rock layers (**strata**) are arranged in the order that they were deposited (unless they have been disturbed by geological events. The most recent layers are near the surface and the oldest are at the bottom. Strata from widespread locations can be correlated because a particular stratum at one location is the same age as the same stratum at a different location.

Profile with Sedimentary Rocks Containing Fossils

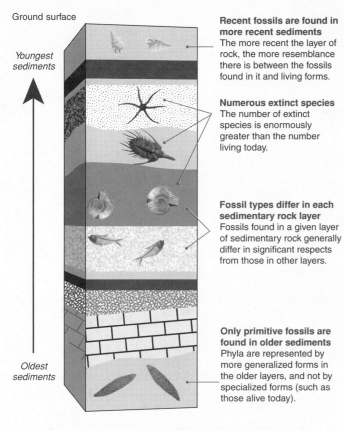

Recent fossils are found in more recent sediments
The more recent the layer of rock, the more resemblance there is between the fossils found in it and living forms.

Numerous extinct species
The number of extinct species is enormously greater than the number living today.

Fossil types differ in each sedimentary rock layer
Fossils found in a given layer of sedimentary rock generally differ in significant respects from those in other layers.

Only primitive fossils are found in older sediments
Phyla are represented by more generalized forms in the older layers, and not by specialized forms (such as those alive today).

New fossil types mark changes in environment
In the rocks marking the end of one geological period, it is common to find many new fossils that become dominant in the next. Each geological period had an environment very different from those before and after. Their boundaries coincided with drastic environmental changes and the appearance of new niches. These produced new selection pressures resulting in new adaptive features in the surviving species, as they responded to the changes.

The rate of evolution can vary

According to the fossil record, rates of evolutionary change seem to vary. There are bursts of species formation and long periods of relative stability within species (stasis). The occasional rapid evolution of new forms apparent in the fossil record, is probably a response to a changing environment. During periods of stable environmental conditions, evolutionary change may slow down.

The Fossil Record of Proboscidea

African and Indian elephants have descended from a diverse group of animals known as **proboscideans** (named for their long trunks). The first pig-sized, trunkless members of this group lived in Africa 40 million years ago. From Africa, their descendants invaded all continents except Antarctica and Australia. As the group evolved, they became larger; an effective evolutionary response to deter predators. Examples of extinct members of this group are illustrated below:

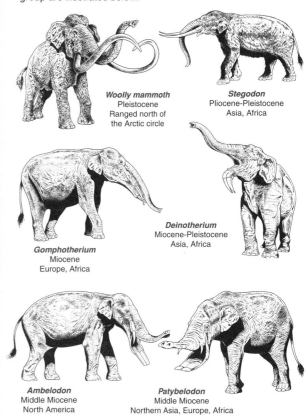

Woolly mammoth Pleistocene Ranged north of the Arctic circle

Stegodon Pliocene-Pleistocene Asia, Africa

Gomphotherium Miocene Europe, Africa

Deinotherium Miocene-Pleistocene Asia, Africa

Ambelodon Middle Miocene North America

Patybelodon Middle Miocene Northern Asia, Europe, Africa

- **Modern day species can be traced:** The evolution of many present-day species can be very well reconstructed. For instance, the evolutionary history of the modern elephants is exceedingly well documented for the last 40 million years. The modern horse also has a well understood fossil record spanning the last 50 million years.

- **Fossil species are similar to but differ from today's species:** Most fossil animals and plants belong to the same major taxonomic groups as organisms living today. However, they do differ from the living species in many features.

1. Name an animal or plant taxon (e.g. family, genus, or species) that has:

(a) A good fossil record of evolutionary development: _____

(b) Appeared to have changed very little over the last 100 million years or so: _____

2. Discuss the importance of **fossils** as a record of evolutionary change over time: _____

© BIOZONE International 2006-2012
ISBN: 978-1-877462-98-6
Photocopying Prohibited

Periodicals: How old is... The quick and the dead

Related activities: Dating Fossils
Weblinks: Getting into the Fossil Record, 29+ Evidences for Macroevolution

RA 2

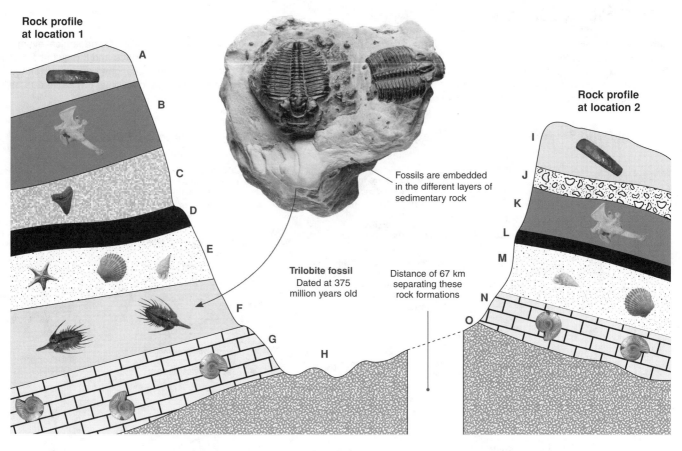

Rock profile at location 1

A
B
C
D
E
F
G
H

Rock profile at location 2

I
J
K
L
M
N
O

Fossils are embedded in the different layers of sedimentary rock

Trilobite fossil
Dated at 375 million years old

Distance of 67 km separating these rock formations

The questions below relate to the diagram above, showing a hypothetical rock profile from two locations separated by a distance of 67 km. There are some differences between the rock layers at the two locations. Apart from layers D and L which are volcanic ash deposits, all other layers comprise sedimentary rock.

3. Assuming there has been no geological activity (e.g. tilting or folding), state in which rock layer (A-O) you would find:

   (a) The youngest rocks at Location 1: _____   (c) The youngest rocks at Location 2: _____

   (b) The oldest rocks at Location 1: _____   (d) The oldest rocks at Location 2: _____

4. (a) State which layer at location 1 is of the same age as layer M at location 2: _____

   (b) Explain the reason for your answer above: _____

   _____

5. The rocks in layer H and O are sedimentary rocks. Explain why there are no visible fossils in layers:

   _____

   _____

6. (a) State which layers present at location 1 are missing at location 2: _____

   (b) State which layers present at location 2 are missing at location 1: _____

7. Describe three methods of dating rocks: _____

   _____

   _____

8. Using radiometric dating, the trilobite fossil was determined to be approximately 375 million years old. The volcanic rock layer (D) was dated at 270 million years old, while rock layer B was dated at 80 million years old. Give the approximate **age range** (i.e. greater than, less than, or between given dates) of the rock layers listed below:

   (a) Layer A: _____   (d) Layer G: _____

   (b) Layer C: _____   (e) Layer L: _____

   (c) Layer E: _____   (f) Layer O: _____

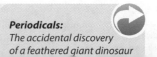

Periodicals:
The accidental discovery
of a feathered giant dinosaur

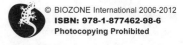

© BIOZONE International 2006-2012
ISBN: 978-1-877462-98-6
Photocopying Prohibited

Dating Fossils

Radiometric dating methods allows an **absolute date** to be assigned to fossils, usually by dating the rocks around the fossils. In the early days of developing these techniques, there were problems in producing dependable results, but the methods have been refined and often now provide dates with a high degree of certainty. Multiple dating methods for samples provides cross-referencing, which gives further confidence in a given date. Absolute, or **chronometric**, dating methods most often involve radiometric dating (e.g. **radiocarbon**, **potassium-argon**, **fission track**), which relies on the radioactive decay of an element. Non-radiometric methods (e.g. **tree-rings**, **paleomagnetism**) can be used in certain specific circumstances.

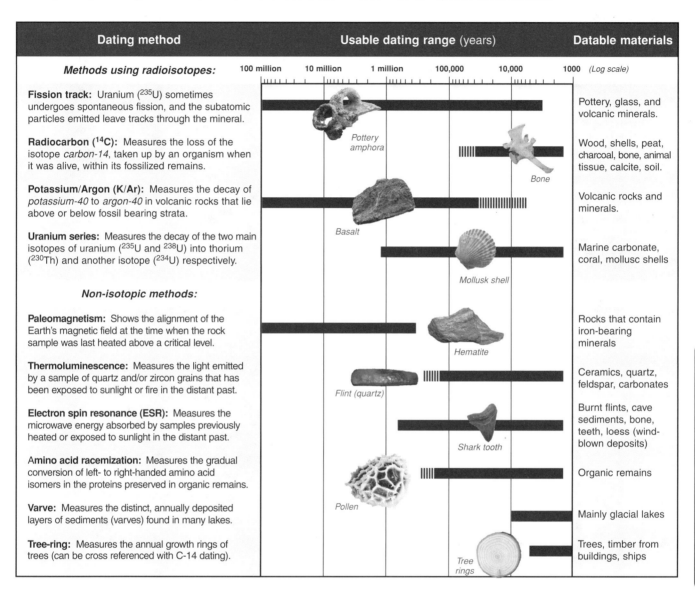

1. Examine the diagram above and determine the approximate dating range (note the logarithmic time scale) and datable materials for each of the methods listed below:

	Dating Range	Datable Materials

(a) Potassium-argon method: _____ _____

(b) Radiocarbon method: _____ _____

(c) Tree-ring method: _____ _____

(d) Thermoluminescence: _____ _____

2. When the date of a sample has been determined, it is common practice to express it in the following manner:
Example: **1.88 ± 0.02** million years old. Explain what the **± 0.02** means in this case:

_____

3. Suggest a possible source of error that could account for an incorrect dating measurement using a radioisotope method:

_____

The Evidence for Evolution

DNA Homologies

Establishing a phylogeny on the basis of homology in a protein, such as cytochrome *c*, is valuable, but it is also analogous to trying to see a complete picture through a small window. The technique of **DNA-DNA hybridization** provides a way to compare the entire genomes of different species by measuring the degree of genetic similarity between pools of DNA sequences. It has been used to determine the genetic distance between two species; the more closely two species are related,

the fewer differences there will be between their genomes. This is because there has been less time for the point mutations that will bring about these differences to occur. This technique gives a measure of 'relatedness', and can be calibrated as a **molecular clock** against known fossil dates. It has been applied to primate DNA samples to help determine the approximate date of human divergence from the apes, which has been estimated to be between 10 and 5 million years ago.

DNA Hybridization

1. DNA from the two species to be compared is extracted, purified and cut into short fragments (e.g. 600-800 base pairs).

2. The DNA of one species is mixed with the DNA of another.

3. The mixture is incubated to allow DNA strands to dissociate and rejoin (anneal), forming hybrid double-stranded DNA.

4. The hybridized sequences that are highly similar will bind more firmly. A measure of the heat energy required to separate the hybrid strands provides a measure of DNA relatedness.

DNA Homologies Today

DNA-DNA hybridization has been criticized because duplicated sequences within a single genome make it unreliable for comparisons between closely related species.

Today, DNA sequencing and computed comparisons are more widely used to compare genomes, although DNA-DNA hybridization is still used to help identify bacteria.

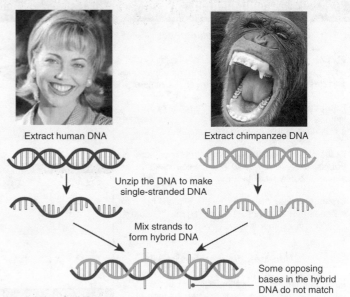
Extract human DNA — Extract chimpanzee DNA. Unzip the DNA to make single-stranded DNA. Mix strands to form hybrid DNA. Some opposing bases in the hybrid DNA do not match

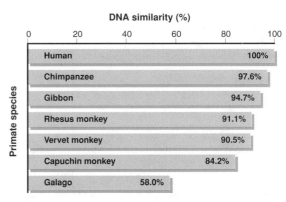

The relationships among the New World vultures and storks have been determined using DNA hybridization. It has been possible to estimate how long ago various members of the group shared a common ancestor.

Similarity of human DNA to that of other primates

Primate species	DNA similarity (%)
Human	100%
Chimpanzee	97.6%
Gibbon	94.7%
Rhesus monkey	91.1%
Vervet monkey	90.5%
Capuchin monkey	84.2%
Galago	58.0%

The genetic relationships among the primates has been investigated using DNA hybridization. Human DNA was compared with that of the other primates. It largely confirmed what was suspected from anatomical evidence.

1. Explain how **DNA hybridization** can give a measure of genetic relatedness between species:

2. Study the graph showing the results of a DNA hybridization between human DNA and that of other primates.

   (a) Which is the most closely related primate to humans?

   (b) Which is the most distantly related primate to humans?

3. State the DNA difference score for: (a) Shoebills and pelicans:_____ (b) Storks and flamingos: _____

4. On the basis of DNA hybridization, state how long ago the ibises and New World vultures shared a common ancestor:

© BIOZONE International 2006-2012
ISBN: 978-1-877462-98-6
Photocopying Prohibited

Protein Homologies

Traditionally, phylogenies were based largely on anatomical or behavioral traits and biologists attempted to determine the relationships between organisms based on overall degree of similarity or by tracing the appearance of key characteristics. With the advent of molecular techniques, homologies can now be studied at the molecular level as well and these can be compared to the phylogenies established using other methods. Protein sequencing provides an excellent tool for establishing **homologies** (similarities resulting from shared ancestry). Each

protein has a specific number of amino acids arranged in a specific order. Any differences in the sequence reflect changes in the DNA sequence. Commonly studied proteins include blood proteins, such as **hemoglobin** (below), and the respiratory protein **cytochrome *c*** (overleaf). Many of these proteins are highly conserved, meaning they change very little over time, presumably because mutations would be detrimental to basic function. Conservation of protein sequences is indicated by the identical amino acid residues at corresponding parts of proteins.

Amino Acid Differences in Hemoglobin

Human beta chain	0
Chimpanzee	0
Gorilla	1
Gibbon	2
Rhesus monkey	8
Squirrel monkey	9
Dog	15
Horse, cow	25
Mouse	27
Gray kangaroo	38
Chicken	45
Frog	67

When the sequence of the **beta hemoglobin chain** (right), which is 146 amino acids long, is compared between humans, five other primates, and six other vertebrates, the results support the phylogenies established using other methods. The numbers in the table (left) represent the number of amino acid differences between the beta chain of humans and those of other species. In general, the number of amino acid differences between the hemoglobins of different vertebrates is inversely proportional to genetic relatedness.

Shading indicates (from top) primates, non-primate placental mammals, marsupials, and non-mammals.

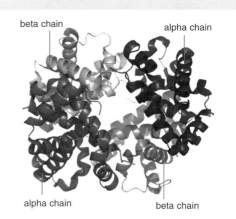

In most vertebrates, the oxygen-transporting blood protein hemoglobin is composed of four polypeptide chains, two alpha chains and two beta chains. Hemoglobin is derived from myoglobin, and ancestral species had just myoglobin for oxygen transport. When the amino acid sequences of myoglobin, the hemoglobin alpha chain, and the hemoglobin beta chain are compared, there are several amino acids that remain conserved between all three. These amino acid sequences must be essential for function because they have remained unchanged throughout evolution.

Using Immunology to Determine Phylogeny

The immune system of one species will recognize the blood proteins of another species as foreign and form antibodies against them. This property can be used to determine the extent of homology between species. Blood proteins, such as albumins, are used to prepare **antiserum** in rabbits. The antiserum contains antibodies against the test blood proteins (e.g. human) and will react to those proteins in any blood sample they are mixed with. The extent of the reaction indicates how different the proteins are; the greater the reaction, the greater the homology. This principle is illustrated (right) for antiserum produced to human blood and its reaction with the blood of other primates and a rat.

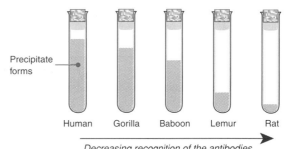

Decreasing recognition of the antibodies against human blood proteins

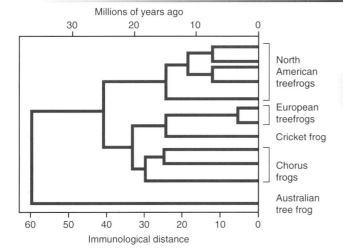

The relationships among tree frogs have been established by immunological studies based on blood proteins such as immunoglobulins and albumins. The **immunological distance** is a measure of the number of amino acid substitutions between two groups. This, in turn, has been calibrated to provide a time scale showing when the various related groups diverged.

© BIOZONE International 2006-2012
ISBN: 978-1-877462-98-6
Photocopying Prohibited

Related activities: DNA Homologies
Weblinks: Evidence for Evolution

DA 2

Cytochrome *c* and the Molecular Clock Theory

Evolutionary change at the molecular level occurs primarily through fixation of neutral mutations by genetic drift. The rate at which one neutral mutation replaces another depends on the mutation rate, which is fairly constant for any particular gene.

If the rate at which a protein evolves is roughly constant over time, the amount of molecular change that a protein shows can be used as a molecular clock to date evolutionary events, such as the divergence of species.

The molecular clock for each species, and each protein, may run at different rates, so scientists calibrate the molecular clock data with other evidence (morphological, molecular) to confirm phylogenetic relationships.

For example, 20 amino acid substitutions in a protein since two organisms diverged from a known common ancestor 400 mya indicates an average substitution rate of 5 substitutions per 100 my.

	1					6				10				14			17	18		20		
Human	Gly	Asp	Val	Glu	Lys	Gly	Lys	Lys	Ile	Phe	Ile	Met	Lys	**Cys**	Ser	Gln	**Cys**	His	Thr	Val	Glu	Lys
Pig											Val	Gln			Ala							
Chicken			Ile								Val	Gln										
Dogfish									Val		Val	Gln			Ala							Asn
Drosophila	<<								Leu		Val	Gln	Arg		Ala							Ala
Wheat	<<	Asn	Pro	Asp	Ala		Ala				Lys	Thr			Ala						Asp	Ala
Yeast	<<	Ser	Ala	Lys			Ala	Thr	Leu		Lys	Thr	Arg			Glu	Leu					

This table shows the N-terminal 22 amino acid residues of human cytochrome *c*, with corresponding sequences from other organisms aligned beneath. Sequences are aligned to give the most position matches. A shaded square indicates no change. In every case, the cytochrome's heme group is attached to the Cys-14 and Cys-17. In *Drosophila*, wheat, and yeast, arrows indicate that several amino acids precede the sequence shown.

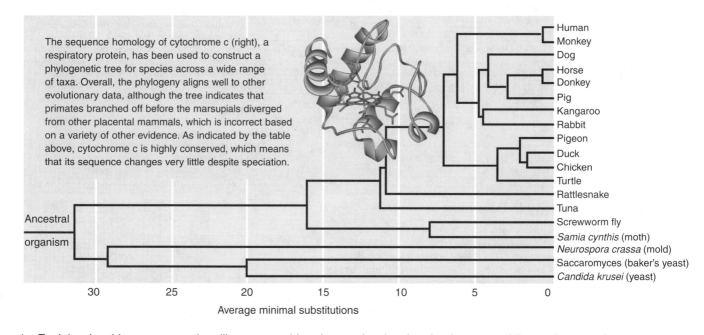

The sequence homology of cytochrome c (right), a respiratory protein, has been used to construct a phylogenetic tree for species across a wide range of taxa. Overall, the phylogeny aligns well to other evolutionary data, although the tree indicates that primates branched off before the marsupials diverged from other placental mammals, which is incorrect based on a variety of other evidence. As indicated by the table above, cytochrome c is highly conserved, which means that its sequence changes very little despite speciation.

1. Explain why chimpanzees and gorillas are considered most closely related to humans, while monkeys are less so:

   _____

2. (a) Why would a respiratory protein like cytochrome C be highly conserved? _____

   _____

   (b) Why are highly conserved proteins good candidates for use in establishing protein homologies? _____

   _____

   _____

3. Discuss some of the limitations of using protein homology, specifically molecular clocks, to establish phylogeny:

   _____

   _____

   _____

The Evolution of Novel Forms

The relatively new field of **evolutionary developmental biology** (or evo-devo) addresses the origin and evolution of embryonic development and looks at how modifications of developmental processes can lead to novel features. Scientists now know that specific genes in animals, including a subgroup of genes called **Hox genes**, are part of a basic **'tool kit'** of genes that control animal development. Genomic studies have shown

that these genes are **highly conserved** (i.e. they show little change in different lineages). Very disparate organisms share the same **tool kit** of genes, but regulate them differently. The implication of this is that large changes in morphology or function are associated with changes in gene regulation, rather than the evolution of new genes, and natural selection associated with gene switches plays a major role in evolution.

The Role of *Hox* Genes

Hox genes control the development of back and front parts of the body. The same genes (or homologous ones) are present in essentially all animals, including humans.

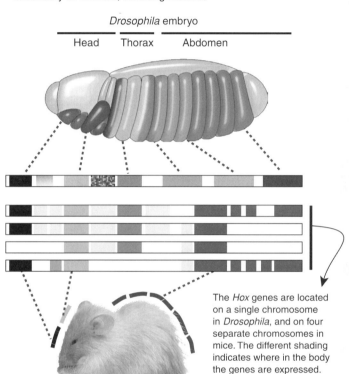

Drosophila embryo

Head   Thorax   Abdomen

The *Hox* genes are located on a single chromosome in *Drosophila*, and on four separate chromosomes in mice. The different shading indicates where in the body the genes are expressed.

The Evolution of Novel Forms

Even very small changes (mutations) in the *Hox* genes can have a profound effect on morphology. Such changes to the genes controlling development have almost certainly been important in the evolution of novel structures and body plans. Four principles underlie the role of developmental genes in the evolution of novel forms:

- **Evolution works with what is already present**: New structures are modifications of pre-existing structures.

- **Multifunctionality** and **redundancy**: Functional redundancy in any part of a multifunctional structure allows for specialization and division of labor through the development of two separate structures.

  Example: the diversity of appendages (including mouthparts) in arthropods.

- **Modularity**: Modular architecture in animals (arthropods, vertebrates) allows for the modification and specialization of individual body parts. Genetic switches allow changes in one part of a structure, independent of other parts.

The Evidence for Evolution

Shifting *Hox* Expression

Huge diversity in morphology in organisms within and across phyla could have arisen through small changes in the genes controlling development.

Differences in neck length in vertebrates provides a good example of how changes in gene expression can bring about changes in morphology. Different vertebrates have different numbers of neck vertebrae. The boundary between neck and trunk vertebrae is marked by expression of the **Hox c6** gene (c6 denotes the sixth cervical or neck vertebra) in all cases, but the position varies in each animal relative to the overall body. The forelimb (arrow) arises at this boundary in all four-legged vertebrates. In snakes, the boundary is shifted forward to the base of the skull and no limbs develop. As a result of these differences in expression, mice have a short neck, geese a long neck, and snakes, no neck at all.

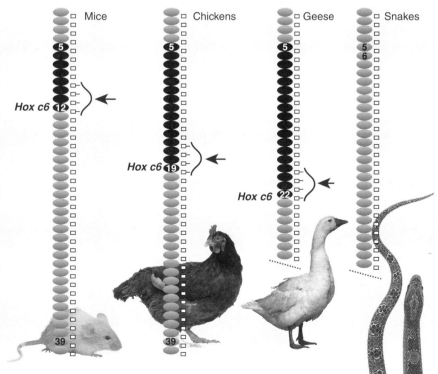

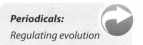

Periodicals:
Regulating evolution

***Related activities**: The Rate of Evolutionary Change*
***Weblinks**: Genetic Tool Kit*

EA 3

Genetic Switches in Evolution

The *Hox* genes are just part of the collection of genes that make up the genetic tool kit for animal development. The genes in the tool kit act as switches, shaping development by affecting how other genes are turned on or off. The distribution of genes in the tool kit indicates that it is ancient and was in place before the evolution of most types of animals. Differences in form arise through changes in genetic switches. One example is the evolution of eyespots in butterflies:

- The **Distal-less** gene is one of the important **master body-building genes** in the genetic tool kit. Switches in the *Distal-less* gene control expression in the embryo (E), larval legs (L), and wing (W) in flies and butterflies, but butterflies have also evolved an extra switch (S) to control eyespot development.

- Once spots evolved, changes in *Distal-less* expression (through changes in the switch) produced more or fewer spots.

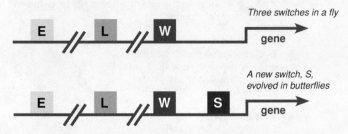

Changes in *Distal-less* regulation were probably achieved by changing specific sequences of the *Distal-less* gene eyespot switch. The result? Changes in eyespot size and number.

Same Gene, New Tricks

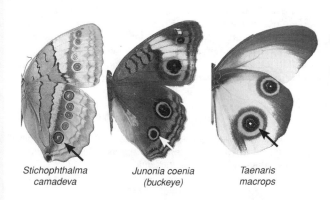

Stichophthalma camadeva   *Junonia coenia (buckeye)*   *Taenaris macrops*

- The action of a tool kit protein depends on context: where particular cells are located at the time when the gene is switched on.

- Changes in the DNA sequence of a genetic switch can change the zone of gene expression without disrupting the function of the tool kit protein itself.

- The spectacular **eyespots** on butterfly wings (arrowed above) represent different degrees of a basic pattern, from virtually all eyespot elements expressed (*Stichophthalma*) to very few (*Taenaris*).

1. Explain what is meant by "evo-devo" and explain its aims: _____

_____

_____

2. Briefly describe the role of *Hox* genes in animal development: _____

_____

_____

_____

3. Outline the evidence that evo-devo provides for evolution and the mechanisms by which it occurs: _____

_____

_____

_____

_____

4. Using an example, discuss how changes in gene expression can bring about changes in morphology:

_____

_____

_____

_____

_____

_____

_____

© BIOZONE International 2006-2012
ISBN: 978-1-877462-98-6
Photocopying Prohibited

Homologous Structures

The evolutionary relationships between groups of organisms is determined mainly by structural similarities called **homologous structures** (homologies), which suggest that they all descended from a common ancestor with that feature. The bones of the forelimb of air-breathing vertebrates are composed of similar bones arranged in a comparable pattern. This is indicative of a common ancestry. The early land vertebrates were amphibians and possessed a limb structure called the **pentadactyl limb**: a limb with five fingers or toes (below left). All vertebrates that descended from these early amphibians, including reptiles, birds and mammals, have limbs that have evolved from this same basic pentadactyl pattern. They also illustrate the phenomenon known as **adaptive radiation**, since the basic limb plan has been adapted to meet the requirements of different niches.

Generalized Pentadactyl Limb

The forelimbs and hind limbs have the same arrangement of bones but they have different names. In many cases bones in different parts of the limb have been highly modified to give it a specialized locomotory function.

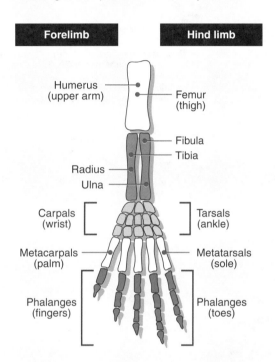

Specializations of Pentadactyl Limbs

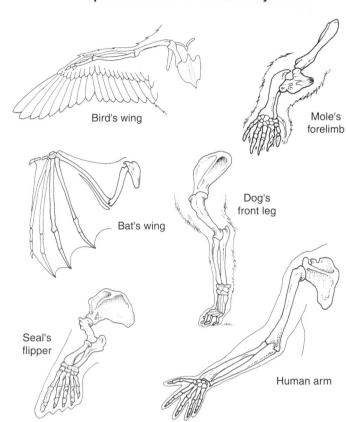

Bird's wing

Mole's forelimb

Bat's wing

Dog's front leg

Seal's flipper

Human arm

The Evidence for Evolution

1. Briefly describe the purpose of the major anatomical change that has taken place in each of the limb examples above:

   (a) Bird wing: _Highly modified for flight. Forelimb is shaped for aerodynamic lift and feather attachment._

   (b) Human arm: _____

   (c) Seal flipper: _____

   (d) Dog foot: _____

   (e) Mole forelimb: _____

   (f) Bat wing: _____

2. Explain how homology in the pentadactyl limb is evidence for adaptive radiation: _____

   _____

   _____

   _____

3. Homology in the behavior of animals (for example, sharing similar courtship or nesting rituals) is sometimes used to indicate the degree of relatedness between groups. How could behavior be used in this way:

   _____

   _____

   _____

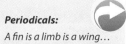
Periodicals:
A fin is a limb is a wing…

Weblinks: *All in the Family, Homologous Structures*

Vestigial Characteristics

Some classes of characters are more valuable than others as reliable indicators of common ancestry. Often, the less any part of an animal is used for specialized purposes, the more important it becomes for classification. This is because common ancestry is easier to detect if a particular feature is unaffected by specific adaptations arising later during the evolution of the species. Vestigial organs are an example of this because, if they have no clear function and they are no longer subject to natural selection, they will remain unchanged through a lineage. It is sometimes argued that some vestigial organs are not truly vestigial, i.e. they may perform some small function. While this may be true in some cases, the features can still be considered vestigial if their new role is a minor one, unrelated to their original function.

Ancestors of Modern Whales

1.8 m long

Pakicetus (early Eocene) a carnivorous, four limbed, early Eocene whale ancestor, probably rather like a large otter. It was still partly terrestrial and not fully adapted for aquatic life.

2.5 m long

Protocetus (mid Eocene). Much more whale-like than *Pakicetus*. The hind limbs were greatly reduced and although they still protruded from the body (arrowed), they were useless for swimming.

20-25 m long

Basilosaurus (late Eocene). A very large ancestor of modern whales. The hind limbs contained all the leg bones, but were vestigial and located entirely within the main body, leaving a tissue flap on the surface (arrowed).

Vestigial organs are common in nature. The vestigial hind limbs of modern whales (right) provide anatomical evidence for their evolution from a carnivorous, four footed, terrestrial ancestor. The oldest known whale, *Pakicetus*, from the early Eocene (~54 mya) still had four limbs. By the late Eocene (~40 mya), whales were fully marine and had lost almost all traces of their former terrestrial life. For fossil evidence, see *Whale Origins* at the weblink below.

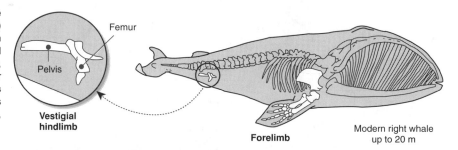

Femur / Pelvis / **Vestigial hindlimb** / **Forelimb** / Modern right whale up to 20 m

RM-DoC

Vestigial organs in birds and reptiles

In all snakes (far left), one lobe of the lung is vestigial (there is not sufficient room in the narrow body cavity for it). In some snakes there are also vestiges of the pelvic girdle and hind limbs of their walking ancestors. Like all ratites, kiwis (left) are flightless. However, more than in other ratites, the wings of kiwis are reduced to tiny vestiges. Kiwis evolved in the absence of predators to a totally ground dwelling existence.

1. In terms of natural selection explain how structures, that were once useful to an organism, could become vestigial:

2. Suggest why a vestigial structure, once it has been reduced to a certain size, may not disappear altogether:

3. Whale evolution shows the presence of **transitional forms** (fossils that are intermediate between modern forms and very early ancestors). Suggest how vestigial structures indicate the common ancestry of these forms:

© BIOZONE International 2006-2012 ISBN: 978-1-877462-98-6 Photocopying Prohibited

Related activities: Homologous Structures
Weblinks: Vestigial Organs, Whale Origins

Periodicals: A waste of space

The Evolution of Horses

The evolution of the horse from the ancestral *Hyracotherium* to modern *Equus* is well documented in the fossil record. For this reason it is often used to illustrate the process of evolution. The rich fossil record, which includes numerous **transitional fossils**, has enabled scientists to develop a robust model of horse phylogeny. Although the evolution of the line was once considered to be a gradual straight line process, it has been radically revised to a complex tree-like lineage with many divergences (below). It showed no inherent direction, and a diverse array of species coexisted for some time over the 55 million year evolutionary period. The environmental transition from forest to grasslands drove many of the changes observed in the equid fossil record. These include reduction in toe number, increased size of cheek teeth, lengthening of the face, and increasing body size.

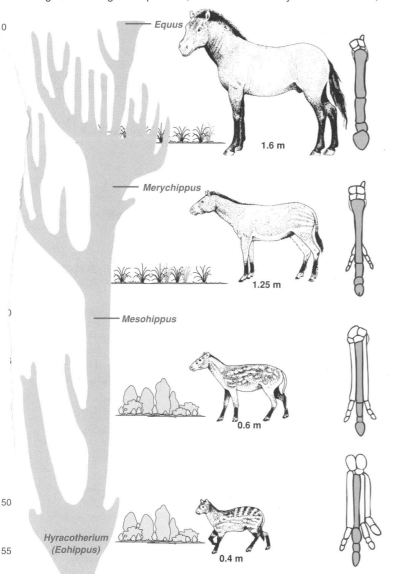

Equus — 1.6 m
Merychippus — 1.25 m
Mesohippus — 0.6 m
Hyracotherium (Eohippus) — 0.4 m

The cooler climates that prevailed in the Miocene (23 -5 mya) brought about a reduction in forested areas with grasslands becoming more abundant. The change in vegetation resulted in the equids developing more durable teeth to cope with the harsher diet. Over time the equid molar became longer and squarer with a hard cement-like covering to enable them to grind the grasses which became their primary diet.

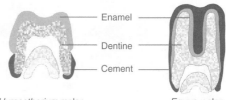

Enamel — Dentine — Cement

Hyracotherium molar   *Equus* molar

The equids also became taller and faster to enable them to view and escape their predators. This is evident in their overall increase in size and the elongation of their limbs. The reduction in the number of toes from four to one (left) also enabled them to run faster and more efficiently.

The majority of equid evolution took place in North America, although now extinct species did migrate to other areas of the globe at various times. During the late Pliocene (2.6 mya) *Equus* spread into the old world and diversified into several species including the modern zebra of Africa and the true horse, *Equus caballus*. Ironically, the horse became extinct in the Americas about 11,000 years ago, and was reintroduced in the 16th century by Spanish explorers.

1. Explain how the environmental change from forest to grassland influenced the following aspects of equid evolution:

   (a) Change in tooth structure: _____

   _____

   (b) Limb length: _____

   _____

   (c) Reduction in number of toes: _____

   _____

2. In which way does the equid fossil record provide a good example of the evolutionary process? _____

   _____

   _____

   _____

© BIOZONE International 2006-2012
ISBN: 978-1-877462-98-6
Photocopying Prohibited

Related activities: History of Life on Earth, Fossil Formation
Weblinks: Horse Evolution, Fossil Horse Cybermuseum

KEY TERMS: Mix and Match

INSTRUCTIONS: Test your vocabulary by matching each term to its definition, as identified by its preceding letter code.

biogeography	**A** The record of life on Earth, preserved in fossils.
chronometric dating	**B** A division of a geologic period. The Miocene and Eocene are examples.
	C The study relating the evolution of new characteristics to changes in the genes controlling development. Evolutionary developmental biology (acronym).
common ancestor	**D** The study of similarities and differences in the anatomy of organisms.
comparative anatomy	**E** Structures in different but related species that are derived from the same ancestral structure but now serve different purposes, e.g. wings and fins..
epoch	**F** A clearly defined period of time that is of an arbitrary but well defined length, and is marked by a start event and an end event. A division of an eon.
evo-devo	**G** The preserved remains or traces (e.g. footprints) of past organisms.
fossil	**H** A technique used to date rocks and other material, based on comparing the relative abundances of a radioactive isotope and its decay products, using known decay rates.
fossil record	**I** The study of how biodiversity is distributed over space and time.
geologic era	**J** The process of determining specific date for an archeological or paleontological site or artifact, usually based on its physical or chemical properties. Also called absolute dating.
geologic period	**K** A method that determines the sequential order in which past events occurred, without necessarily determining their absolute age. Also called chronostatic dating.
geologic time scale	**L** A method, analogous to a timepiece, that uses molecular change to deduce the time in geologic history when two taxa diverged and so can be used to establish phylogenies.
homologous structures	**M** A division of a geologic era. The Jurassic and Triassic are examples.
Hox genes	**N** A layer of sedimentary rock or soil with characteristics that distinguish it from other layers. It is the basic unit in a stratigraphic column.
molecular clock	**O** The evolutionary history or genealogy of a group of organisms. Often represented as a 'tree' showing descent of new species from the ancestral one..
paleontology	**P** A historical science involving the study of prehistoric life, including the evolution of organisms.
phylogeny	**Q** A system of chronological measurement relating stratigraphy to time. It is used by scientists to describe the timing and relationships between events in the history of the Earth.
radiometric dating	**R** The fossilized remains organisms that illustrate an evolutionary transition in that they possess both primitive and derived characteristics.
relative dating	**S** Genes that play a role in development and are shared by almost all organisms.
rock strata	**T** Homologous characters (including anatomical structures, behaviors, and biochemical pathways) that have apparently lost all or most of their original function in a species through evolution.
transitional fossil	**U** The (usually most recent) individual from which all organisms within a taxon are directly descended.
vestigial structure	

The Mechanisms of Evolution

Key terms

adaptation
allele frequency
allopatric (allopatry)
balanced polymorphism
Darwin
deme
differential survival
directional selection
disruptive selection
evolution
fitness
fixation (of alleles)
founder effect
gene flow
gene pool
genetic bottleneck
genetic drift
genetic equilibrium
Hardy-Weinberg equation
heterozygous advantage
industrial melanism
mate choice
microevolution
migration
mutation
natural selection
population
postzygotic isolating
    mechanism
prezygotic isolating
    mechanism
reproductive isolation
ring species
selection pressure
speciation
species
stabilizing selection
sub-species
sympatric (sympatry)

Periodicals:
Listings for this
chapter are on page 122

Weblinks:
www.thebiozone.com/
weblink/Evol-2986.html

Presentation Media
EVOLUTION:
Population Genetics, Evolution

Key concepts

▶ Evolution (change in allele frequencies in a gene pool) is a consequence of populations rarely being in genetic equilibrium.

▶ It is possible to calculate allele frequencies for a population.

▶ Reproductive isolation is essential for speciation. This is often preceded by allopatry.

▶ Natural selection sorts the variability in gene pools and establishes adaptive genotypes.

Objectives

☐ 1. Use the **KEY TERMS** to help you understand and complete these objectives.

The Modern Synthesis of Evolution   pages 38-41

☐ 2. Explain what is meant by biological **evolution**. Outline Darwin's *"Theory of evolution by natural selection"* and explain how it has been modified in the **new synthesis** to account our current understanding of genetics.

☐ 3. Explain what is meant by **fitness** and discuss how evolution through **adaptation** equips species for survival. Describe structural, behavioral, and physiological adaptations of organisms to their environment.

Species and Gene Pools   pages 42-70

☐ 4. Explain what is meant by a (biological) **species** and describe the limitations of its definition. Explain **ring species** and their significance.

☐ 5. Understand the concept of the **gene pool** and explain the term **deme**. Explain how **allele frequencies** are expressed for populations.

☐ 6. State the conditions required for **genetic equilibrium** in a population and explain the consequences of these conditions rarely, if ever, being satisfied. Use the **Hardy-Weinberg equation** to calculate allele frequencies, genotype frequencies, and phenotype frequencies for a gene in a population.

☐ 7. Explain how each of the following processes alters allele frequencies in a gene pool: **natural selection**, **genetic drift**, **gene flow**, and **mutation**.

☐ 8. Explain the role of **natural selection** in sorting the variability within a gene pool and establishing adaptive genotypes. Explain **stabilizing**, **directional**, and **disruptive selection**. Describe examples of evolution by **natural selection**.

☐ 9. Explain the genetic and evolutionary consequences of the **founder effect**.

☐ 10. Explain the genetic and evolutionary consequences of the **bottleneck effect**.

Speciation   pages 72-78

☐ 11. Explain the difference between **allopatric** and **sympatric** populations.

☐ 12. Explain **allopatric speciation** in terms of **migration**, geographical **isolation**, and **adaptation** leading to reproductive or genetic isolation of gene pools.

☐ 13. Describe and explain mechanisms of **reproductive isolation**, distinguishing between **prezygotic** and **postzygotic** reproductive isolating mechanisms.

☐ 14. Describe and explain **sympatric speciation** and discuss the role of **polyploidy** in **instant speciation** events.

☐ 15. Describe stages in species development, including reference to the reduction in **gene flow** as populations become increasingly isolated.

Genes, Inheritance, and Evolution

Each individual is the carrier of its own particular combination of alleles. In sexually reproducing organisms, different allele combinations arise because of the events occurring in meiosis and fertilization, and as a result of mate selection. Some combinations are well suited to the prevailing environment, while others are less so. Organisms with favorable allele combinations will have greater reproductive success (**fitness**) than those with less favorable allele combinations. Consequently, their alleles will be represented in greater proportion in subsequent generations. For asexual organisms, offspring are essentially clones, but (as in sexually reproducing organisms) new alleles can arise through mutation and some of these may confer a selective advantage. Of course, environments are rarely static, so new allele combinations are constantly being tested for success. Natural selection sorts the variation present to establish phenotypes that are adaptive in the environment of the time.

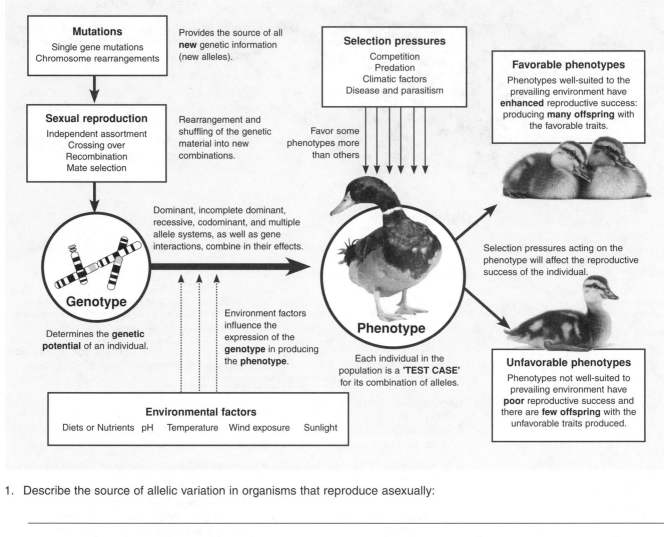

1. Describe the source of allelic variation in organisms that reproduce asexually:

_____

_____

2. Explain why each individual in a population is a **test case** for its combination of alleles: _____

_____

_____

_____

_____

_____

3. Discuss the role of sexual reproduction and mutation in providing the raw material for selecting favorable phenotypes:

_____

_____

_____

_____

Weblinks: *Variation: Snails*

© BIOZONE International 2006-2012
ISBN: 978-1-877462-98-6
Photocopying Prohibited

Adaptation and Fitness

An **adaptation** is any heritable trait that equips an organism to its functional position in the environment (its niche). These traits may be structural, physiological, or behavioral and reflect ancestry as well as adaptation. Adaptation is important in an evolutionary sense because adaptive features promote fitness. **Fitness** is a measure of an organism's ability to maximize the numbers of offspring surviving to reproductive age. Genetic adaptation must not be confused with **physiological adjustment** (acclimatization), which refers to an organism's ability to adapt during its lifetime to changing environmental conditions (e.g. a person's acclimatization to altitude). Examples of adaptive features arising through evolution are illustrated below.

Ear Length in Rabbits and Hares

The external ears of many mammals are used as important organs to assist in thermoregulation (controlling loss and gain of body heat). The ears of rabbits and hares native to hot, dry climates, such as the jack rabbit of south-western USA and northern Mexico, are relatively very large. The Arctic hare lives in the tundra zone of Alaska, northern Canada and Greenland, and has ears that are relatively short. This reduction in the size of the extremities (ears, limbs, and noses) is typical of cold adapted species.

Arctic hare: *Lepus arcticus*

Black-tail jackrabbit: *Lepus californicus*

Body Size in Relation to Climate

Regulation of body temperature requires a large amount of energy and mammals exhibit a variety of structural and physiological adaptations to increase the effectiveness of this process. Heat production in any endotherm depends on body volume (heat generating metabolism), whereas the rate of heat loss depends on surface area. Increasing body size minimizes heat loss to the environment by reducing the surface area to volume ratio. Animals in colder regions therefore tend to be larger overall than those living in hot climates. This relationship is know as **Bergman's rule** and it is well documented in many mammalian species. Cold adapted species also tend to have more compact bodies and shorter extremities than related species in hot climates.

Fennec fox

Arctic fox

The **fennec fox** of the Sahara illustrates the adaptations typical of mammals living in hot climates: a small body size and lightweight fur, and long ears, legs, and nose. These features facilitate heat dissipation and reduce heat gain.

The **Arctic fox** shows the physical characteristics typical of cold-adapted mammals: a stocky, compact body shape with small ears, short legs and nose, and dense fur. These features reduce heat loss to the environment.

Number of Horns in Rhinoceroses

Not all differences between species can be convincingly interpreted as adaptations to particular environments. Rhinoceroses charge rival males and predators, and the horn(s), when combined with the head-down posture, add effectiveness to this behavior. Horns are obviously adaptive, but it is not clear if having one (Indian rhino) or two (black rhino) horns is related to the functionality in the environment or a reflection of divergence from a small hornless ancestor.

Great Indian rhino

African black rhino

1. Distinguish between adaptive features (genetic) and acclimatization: _____

_____

_____

2. Explain the nature of the relationship between the length of extremities (such as limbs and ears) and climate:

_____

_____

3. Explain the adaptive value of a larger body size at high latitude: _____

_____

_____

The Mechanisms of Evolution

© BIOZONE International 2006-2012
ISBN: 978-1-877462-98-6
Photocopying Prohibited

Related activities: Genes, Inheritance, and Evolution

Weblinks: Adaptation

A 2

The Modern Theory of Evolution

Although **Charles Darwin** is credited with the development of the theory of evolution by natural selection, there were many people that contributed ideas upon which he built his own. Since Darwin first proposed his theory, aspects that were problematic (such as the mechanism of inheritance) have now been explained. The development of the modern theory of evolution has a history going back at least two centuries. The diagram below illustrates the way in which some of the major contributors helped to form the currently accepted model, or **new synthesis**. Understanding of evolutionary processes continued to grow through the 1980s and 1990s as comparative molecular sequence data were amassed and understanding of the molecular basis of developmental mechanisms improved. Most recently, in the exciting new area of evolutionary developmental biology (**evo-devo**), biologists have been exploring how developmental gene expression patterns explain how groups of organisms evolved.

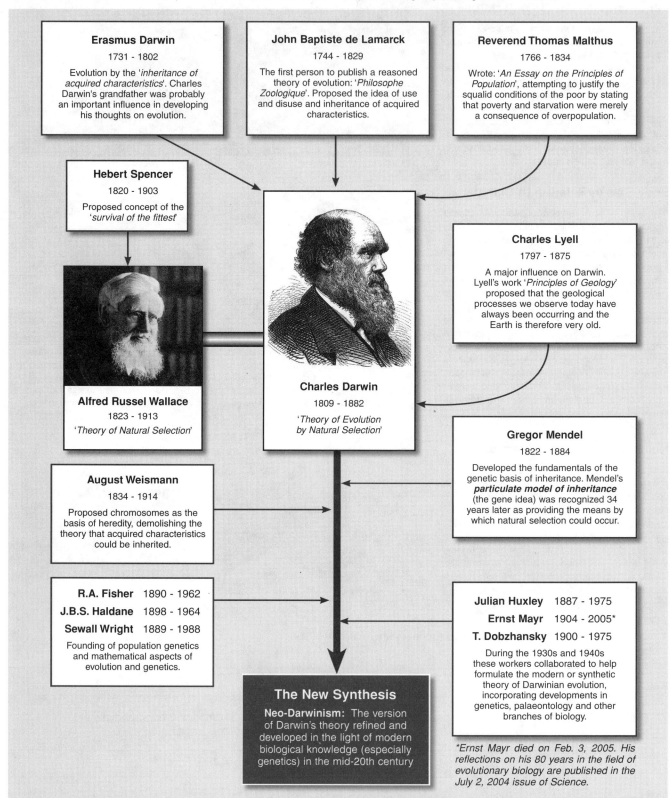

Erasmus Darwin

1731 - 1802

Evolution by the '*inheritance of acquired characteristics*'. Charles Darwin's grandfather was probably an important influence in developing his thoughts on evolution.

John Baptiste de Lamarck

1744 - 1829

The first person to publish a reasoned theory of evolution: '*Philosophe Zoologique*'. Proposed the idea of use and disuse and inheritance of acquired characteristics.

Reverend Thomas Malthus

1766 - 1834

Wrote: '*An Essay on the Principles of Population*', attempting to justify the squalid conditions of the poor by stating that poverty and starvation were merely a consequence of overpopulation.

Hebert Spencer

1820 - 1903

Proposed concept of the '*survival of the fittest*'

Charles Lyell

1797 - 1875

A major influence on Darwin. Lyell's work '*Principles of Geology*' proposed that the geological processes we observe today have always been occurring and the Earth is therefore very old.

Alfred Russel Wallace

1823 - 1913

'*Theory of Natural Selection*'

Charles Darwin

1809 - 1882

'*Theory of Evolution by Natural Selection*'

Gregor Mendel

1822 - 1884

Developed the fundamentals of the genetic basis of inheritance. Mendel's *particulate model of inheritance* (the gene idea) was recognized 34 years later as providing the means by which natural selection could occur.

August Weismann

1834 - 1914

Proposed chromosomes as the basis of heredity, demolishing the theory that acquired characteristics could be inherited.

R.A. Fisher   1890 - 1962
J.B.S. Haldane   1898 - 1964
Sewall Wright   1889 - 1988

Founding of population genetics and mathematical aspects of evolution and genetics.

Julian Huxley   1887 - 1975
Ernst Mayr   1904 - 2005*
T. Dobzhansky   1900 - 1975

During the 1930s and 1940s these workers collaborated to help formulate the modern or synthetic theory of Darwinian evolution, incorporating developments in genetics, palaeontology and other branches of biology.

The New Synthesis

Neo-Darwinism: The version of Darwin's theory refined and developed in the light of modern biological knowledge (especially genetics) in the mid-20th century

Ernst Mayr died on Feb. 3, 2005. His reflections on his 80 years in the field of evolutionary biology are published in the July 2, 2004 issue of Science.

1. From the diagram above, choose one of the contributors to the development of evolutionary theory (excluding Charles Darwin himself), and write a few paragraphs discussing their role in contributing to Darwin's ideas. You may need to consult an encyclopaedia or other reference to assist you.

Related activities: Darwin's Theory, The Evolution of Novel Forms

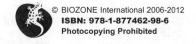

© BIOZONE International 2006-2012
ISBN: 978-1-877462-98-6
Photocopying Prohibited

The Evolution of Darwin's Finches

The Galápagos Islands, off the West coast of Ecuador, comprise 16 main islands and six smaller islands. They are home to a unique range of organisms, including 13 species of finches, each of which is thought to have evolved from a single species of grassquit. After colonizing the islands, the grassquits underwent adaptive radiation in response to the availability of unexploited feeding niches on the islands. This adaptive radiation is most evident in the present beak shape of each species. The beaks are adapted for different purposes such as crushing seeds, pecking wood, or probing flowers for nectar. Current consensus groups the finches into ground finches, tree finches, warbler finches, and the Cocos Island finches. Between them, the 13 species of this endemic group fill the roles of seven different families of South American mainland birds. DNA analyses have confirmed Darwin's insight and have shown that all 13 species evolved from a flock of about 30 birds arriving a million years ago.

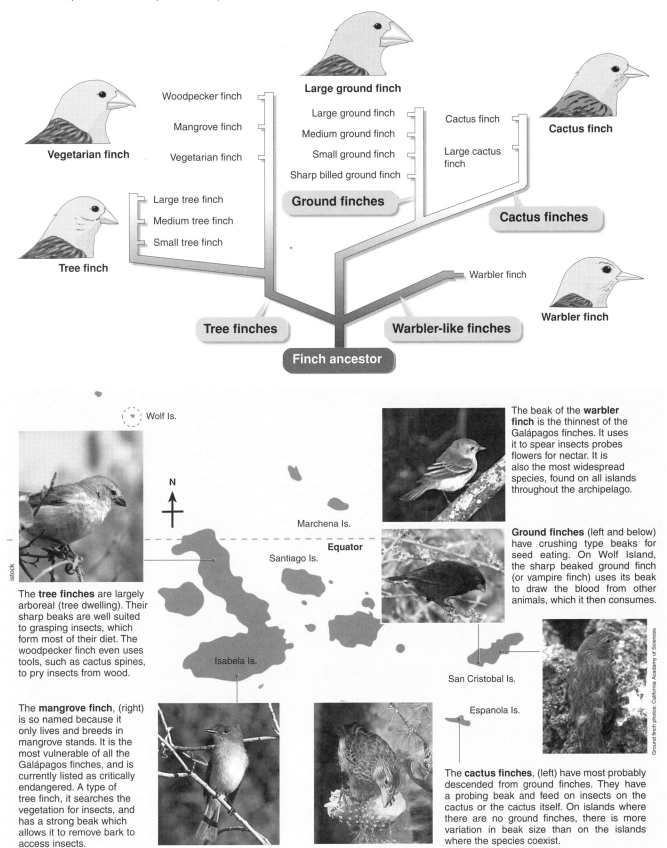

The **tree finches** are largely arboreal (tree dwelling). Their sharp beaks are well suited to grasping insects, which form most of their diet. The woodpecker finch even uses tools, such as cactus spines, to pry insects from wood.

The **mangrove finch**, (right) is so named because it only lives and breeds in mangrove stands. It is the most vulnerable of all the Galápagos finches, and is currently listed as critically endangered. A type of tree finch, it searches the vegetation for insects, and has a strong beak which allows it to remove bark to access insects.

The beak of the **warbler finch** is the thinnest of the Galápagos finches. It uses it to spear insects probes flowers for nectar. It is also the most widespread species, found on all islands throughout the archipelago.

Ground finches (left and below) have crushing type beaks for seed eating. On Wolf Island, the sharp beaked ground finch (or vampire finch) uses its beak to draw the blood from other animals, which it then consumes.

The **cactus finches**, (left) have most probably descended from ground finches. They have a probing beak and feed on insects on the cactus or the cactus itself. On islands where there are no ground finches, there is more variation in beak size than on the islands where the species coexist.

© BIOZONE International 2006-2012
ISBN: 978-1-877462-98-6
Photocopying Prohibited

Related activities: Adaptations and Fitness, Allopatric Speciation
Weblinks: Darwin's Finches

The Mechanisms of Evolution

A 2

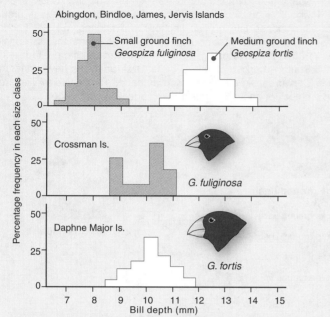

Adaptation in response to resource competition on bill size in small and medium ground finches

Abingdon, Bindloe, James, Jervis Islands

Small ground finch *Geospiza fuliginosa*

Medium ground finch *Geospiza fortis*

Crossman Is.

G. fuliginosa

Daphne Major Is.

G. fortis

Percentage frequency in each size class

Bill depth (mm)

Two species of ground finch *(G. fuliginosa* and *G. fortis)* are found on a number of islands in the Galápagos. On islands where the species occur together, the bill sizes of the two species are quite different and they feed on different sized seeds, thus avoiding direct competition. On islands where each of these species occurs alone, and there is no competition, the bill sizes of both species move to an intermediate range.

Data based on an adaptation by Strickberger (2000)

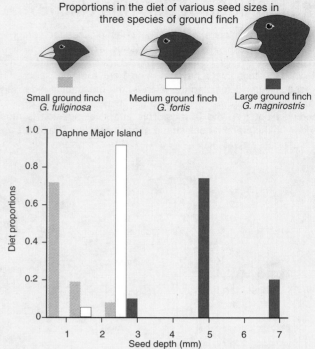

Proportions in the diet of various seed sizes in three species of ground finch

Small ground finch *G. fuliginosa*

Medium ground finch *G. fortis*

Large ground finch *G. magnirostris*

Daphne Major Island

Diet proportions

Seed depth (mm)

Ground finches feed on seeds, but the upper limit of seed size they can handle is constrained by the bill size. Even though small seeds are accessible to all, the birds concentrate on the largest seeds available to them because these provide the most energy for the least handling effort. For example, the large ground finch can easily open smaller seeds, but concentrates on large seeds for their high energy rewards.

1. Describe the main factors that have contributed to the adaptive radiation of Darwin's finches: _____

_____

_____

_____

2. (a) What evidence is there to indicate that species of *Geospiza* compete for the same seed sizes?_____

_____

_____

(b) How have adaptations in bill size enabled coexisting species of *Geospiza* to avoid resource competition?

_____

_____

_____

3. The range of variability shown by a phenotype in response to environmental variation is called **phenotypic plasticity**.

(a) Discuss the evidence for phenotypic plasticity in Galápagos finches: _____

_____

_____

_____

(b) Explain what this suggests about the biology of the original finch ancestor: _____

_____

_____

© BIOZONE International 2006-2012
ISBN: 978-1-877462-98-6
Photocopying Prohibited

Disruptive Selection in Darwin's Finches

The Galápagos Islands are a group of islands 970 km west of Ecuador. They are home to 13 species of finches descended from a common ancestor. The finches have been closely studied over many years. A study during a prolonged drought on Santa Cruz Island showed how **disruptive selection** can change the distribution of genotypes in a population. During the drought, large and small seed sizes were more abundant than the preferred intermediate seed sizes.

Measurements of the beak length, width, and depth were combined into one **single measure**.

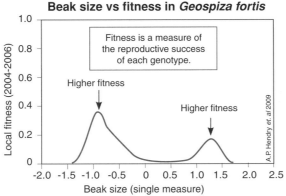

Beak size vs fitness in *Geospiza fortis*

Fitness is a measure of the reproductive success of each genotype.

Higher fitness

Higher fitness

A.P. Hendry et. al 2009

*Fitness showed a **bimodal distribution** (arrowed) being highest for smaller and larger beak sizes.*

Beak sizes of *G. fortis* were measured over a three year period (2004-2006), at the start and end of each year. At the start of the year, individuals were captured, banded, and their beaks were measured.

The presence or absence of banded individuals was recorded at the end of the year when the birds were recaptured. Recaptured individuals had their beaks measured.

The proportion of banded individuals in the population at the end of the year gave a measure of fitness. Absent individuals were presumed dead (fitness = 0).

Fitness related to beak size showed a bimodal distribution (left) typical of disruptive selection.

Beak size pairing in *Geospiza fortis*

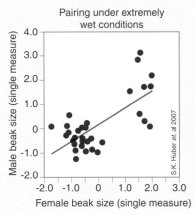

Pairing under extremely wet conditions

S.K. Huber et. al 2007

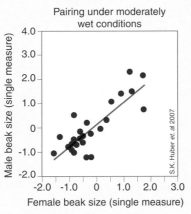

Pairing under moderately wet conditions

S.K. Huber et. al 2007

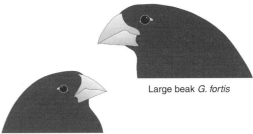

Large beak *G. fortis*

Small beak *G. fortis*

A 2007 study found that breeding pairs of birds had similar beak sizes. Male and females with small beaks tended to breed together, and males and females with large beaks tended to breed together. Mate selection maintained the biomodal distribution in the population during extremely wet conditions. If beak size wasn't a factor in mate selection, the beak size would even out.

1. (a) How did the drought affect seed size on Santa Cruz Island?_____
    _____

    (b) How did the change in seed size during the drought create a selection pressure for changes in beak size?
    _____
    _____
    _____

2. How does beak size relate to fitness (differential reproductive success) in *G. fortis*? _____
    _____
    _____
    _____

3. (a) Is mate selection in *G. fortis* random / non-random? (delete one)

    (b) Give reasons for your answer: _____
    _____
    _____

The Mechanisms of Evolution

Related activities: Natural Selection, The Evolution of Darwin's Finches
Weblinks: Darwin's Finches

Black is the New Gray

The North American gray squirrel (*Sciurus carolinensis*) was introduced into the UK in the 19th century. By 1958 it had spread to most of England and Wales, displacing the smaller native red squirrel (*Sciurus vulgaris*). Now, a black variation of the gray squirrel is beginning to displace the original gray variety, and is common in four areas of Britain (below right). Observations suggest the black form is more aggressive than the gray. This behavior may give them a competitive advantage and may provide a characteristic for selection. This would help explain why the numbers of black squirrels are increasing locally.

Most gene mutations are recessive, but the mutation for black coat color shows incomplete dominance. This allows the black variant to spread more rapidly through the population. There are three genotypes for the gray squirrel:

M^GM^G: Gray coat
Two normal gray alleles

M^GM^B: Brown-black coat
One normal gray allele, one mutant black allele

M^BM^B: Jet black coat
Two mutant black alleles

Photo: D. Gordon E. Robertson

The black color (above) results from a major sequence mutation in the MC1R gene which regulates hair and skin color in mammals. The gene controls the amount of the black eumelanin pigment produced.

Black squirrel numbers have rapidly increased in Hertfordshire, Bedfordshire, Huntingdonshire and Cambridgeshire. It is proposed that the genetic development of black coat color affords the black squirrels a competitive advantage over gray variants. Although none have yet been proven, likely advantages include higher levels of aggression than the gray varieties, and the possibility that the females find the black coat more attractive when selecting mates. A Canadian study has shown that black squirrels have a lower basal metabolic rate and lose heat more slowly than gray squirrels. This would benefit the black variant in cold conditions.

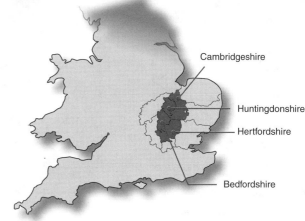

Cambridgeshire

Huntingdonshire

Hertfordshire

Bedfordshire

The Punnett square (right) shows the offspring produced when a gray squirrel (M^GM^G) is mated with brown-black squirrel (M^GM^B). Use it to help you answer the following questions.

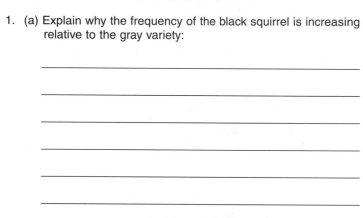

1. (a) Explain why the frequency of the black squirrel is increasing relative to the gray variety:

_____

_____

_____

_____

_____

_____

   (b) Explain what would happen to the rate of change in black squirrel frequency if the mutation for black was recessive:

_____

_____

_____

Related activities: Adaptations and Fitness

Periodicals:
Black squirrels

© BIOZONE International 2006-2012
ISBN: 978-1-877462-98-6
Photocopying Prohibited

Gene Pool Exercise

Cut out each of the beetles on this page and use them to reenact different events within a gene pool as described in this topic

(pages: *Gene Pools and Evolution, Changes in a Gene Pool, The Founder Effect, Population Bottlenecks, Genetic Drift*).

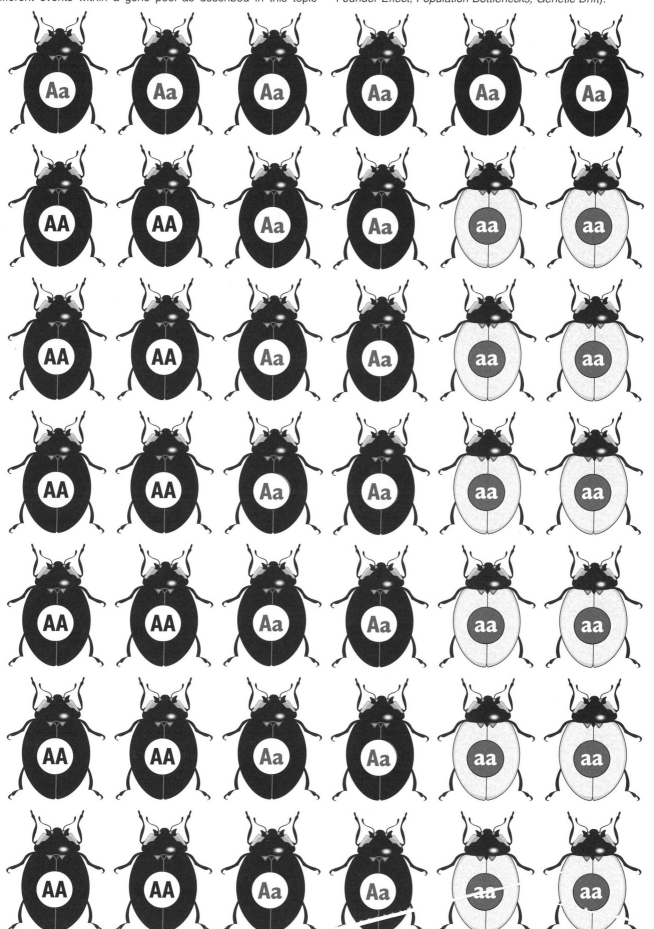

The Mechanisms of Evolution

Related activities: *Gene Pools and Evolution, Changes in a Gene Pool, The Founder Effect, Population Bottlenecks, Genetic Drift*

P

This page has deliberately been left blank

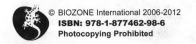

Calculating Allele Frequencies in Populations

The **Hardy-Weinberg equation** provides a simple mathematical model of genetic equilibrium in a gene pool, but its main application in population genetics is in calculating allele and genotype frequencies in populations, particularly as a means of studying changes and measuring their rate. The use of the Hardy-Weinberg equation is described below.

Punnett square

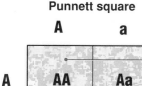

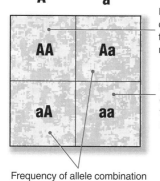

Frequency of allele combination **AA** in the population is represented as p^2

Frequency of allele combination **aa** in the population is represented as q^2

Frequency of allele combination **Aa** in the population (add these together to get **2pq**)

$$(p + q)^2 = p^2 + 2pq + q^2 = 1$$

Frequency of allele types

p = Frequency of allele A

q = Frequency of allele a

Frequency of allele combinations

p^2 = Frequency of AA (homozygous dominant)

2pq = Frequency of Aa (heterozygous)

q^2 = Frequency of aa (homozygous recessive)

How To Solve Hardy-Weinberg Problems

In most populations, the frequency of two alleles of interest is calculated from the proportion of homozygous recessives (q^2), as this is the only genotype identifiable directly from its phenotype. If only the dominant phenotype is known, q^2 may be calculated (1 – the frequency of the dominant phenotype). The following steps outline the procedure for solving a Hardy-Weinberg problem:

Remember that all calculations must be carried out using proportions, NOT PERCENTAGES!

1. Examine the question to determine what piece of information you have been given about the population. In most cases, this is the percentage or frequency of the homozygous recessive phenotype q^2, or the dominant phenotype $p^2 + 2pq$ (see note above).

2. The first objective is to find out the value of p or q, If this is achieved, then every other value in the equation can be determined by simple calculation.

3. Take the square root of q^2 to find q.

4. Determine p by subtracting q from 1 (i.e. p = 1 – q).

5. Determine p^2 by multiplying p by itself (i.e. $p^2 = p \times p$).

6. Determine 2pq by multiplying p times q times 2.

7. Check that your calculations are correct by adding up the values for $p^2 + q^2 + 2pq$ (the sum should equal 1 or 100%).

Worked example

In the American white population approximately 70% of people can taste the chemical phenylthiocarbamide (PTC) (the dominant phenotype), while 30% are non-tasters (the recessive phenotype).

Determine the frequency of:	Answers
(a) Homozygous recessive phenotype(**q^2**).	30% - provided
(b) The dominant allele (**p**).	45.2%
(c) Homozygous tasters (**p^2**).	20.5%
(d) Heterozygous tasters (**2pq**).	49.5%

Data: The frequency of the dominant phenotype (70% tasters) and recessive phenotype (30% non-tasters) are provided.

Working:

Recessive phenotype:	**q^2**	= 30%
		use 0.30 for calculation
therefore:	**q**	= 0.5477
		square root of 0.30
therefore:	**p**	= 0.4523
		1 – q = p
		1 – 0.5477 = 0.4523

Use p and q in the equation (top) to solve any unknown:

Homozygous dominant	**p^2**	= 0.2046
		(p x p = 0.4523 x 0.4523)
Heterozygous:	**2pq**	= 0.4953

---

1. A population of hamsters has a gene consisting of 90% M alleles (black) and 10% m alleles (gray). Mating is random.

   Data: Frequency of recessive allele (10% m) and dominant allele (90% M).

   Determine the proportion of offspring that will be black and the proportion that will be gray (show your working):

   _____

   _____

Recessive allele:	q	=
Dominant allele:	p	=
Recessive phenotype:	q^2	=
Homozygous dominant:	p^2	=
Heterozygous	2pq	=

The Mechanisms of Evolution

Periodicals:
The Hardy-Weinberg principle

Related activities: Analysis of a Squirrel Gene Pool

RDA 2

2. You are working with pea plants and found 36 plants out of 400 were dwarf.
   Data: Frequency of recessive phenotype (36 out of 400 = 9%)

   (a) Calculate the frequency of the tall gene: _____

   (b) Determine the number of heterozygous pea plants:

   _____

   _____

Recessive allele:	q =	
Dominant allele:	p =	
Recessive phenotype:	q^2 =	
Homozygous dominant:	p^2 =	
Heterozygous:	2pq =	

3. In humans, the ability to taste the chemical phenylthiocarbamide (PTC) is inherited as a simple dominant characteristic. Suppose you found out that 360 out of 1000 college students could not taste the chemical.
   Data: Frequency of recessive phenotype (360 out of 1000).

   (a) State the frequency of the gene for tasting PTC:

   _____

   (b) Determine the number of heterozygous students in this population:

   _____

Recessive allele:	q =	
Dominant allele:	p =	
Recessive phenotype:	q^2 =	
Homozygous dominant:	p^2 =	
Heterozygous:	2pq =	

4. A type of deformity appears in 4% of a large herd of cattle. Assume the deformity was caused by a recessive gene.
   Data: Frequency of recessive phenotype (4% deformity).

   (a) Calculate the percentage of the herd that are carriers of the gene:

   _____

   (b) Determine the frequency of the dominant gene in this case:

   _____

Recessive allele:	q =	
Dominant allele:	p =	
Recessive phenotype:	q^2 =	
Homozygous dominant:	p^2 =	
Heterozygous:	2pq =	

5. Assume you placed 50 pure bred black guinea pigs (dominant allele) with 50 albino guinea pigs (recessive allele) and allowed the population to attain genetic equilibrium (several generations have passed).
   Data: Frequency of recessive allele (50%) and dominant allele (50%).

   Determine the proportion (%) of the population that becomes white:

   _____

Recessive allele:	q =	
Dominant allele:	p =	
Recessive phenotype:	q^2 =	
Homozygous dominant:	p^2 =	
Heterozygous:	2pq =	

6. It is known that 64% of a large population exhibit the recessive trait of a characteristic controlled by two alleles (one is dominant over the other).
   Data: Frequency of recessive phenotype (64%). Determine the following:

   (a) The frequency of the recessive allele: _____

   (b) The percentage that are heterozygous for this trait: _____

   (c) The percentage that exhibit the dominant trait: _____

   (d) The percentage that are homozygous for the dominant trait: _____

   (e) The percentage that has one or more recessive alleles: _____

7. Albinism is recessive to normal pigmentation in humans. The frequency of the albino allele was 10% in a population.
   Data: Frequency of recessive allele (10% albino allele).

   Determine the proportion of people that you would expect to be albino:

   _____

   _____

Recessive allele:	q =	
Dominant allele:	p =	
Recessive phenotype:	q^2 =	
Homozygous dominant:	p^2 =	
Heterozygous:	2pq =	

Analysis of a Squirrel Gene Pool

In Olney, Illinois, in the United States, there is a unique population of albino (white) and gray squirrels. Between 1977 and 1990, students at Olney Central College carried out a study of this population. They recorded the frequency of gray and albino squirrels. The albinos displayed a mutant allele expressed as an albino phenotype only in the homozygous recessive condition. The data they collected are provided in the table below. Using the **Hardy-Weinberg equation** for calculating genotype frequencies, it was possible to estimate the frequency of the normal 'wild' allele (G) providing gray fur coloring, and the frequency of the mutant albino allele (g) producing white squirrels. This study provided real, first hand, data that students could use to see how genotype frequencies can change in a real population.

Thanks to **Dr. John Stencel**, Olney Central College, Olney, Illinois, US, for providing the data for this exercise.

Gray squirrel, usual color form

Albino form of gray squirrel

Population of gray and white squirrels in Olney, Illinois (1977-1990)

Year	Gray	White	Total	GG	Gg	gg	Freq. of g	Freq. of G
1977	602	182	784	26.85	49.93	23.21	48.18	51.82
1978	511	172	683	24.82	50.00	25.18	50.18	49.82
1979	482	134	616	28.47	49.77	21.75	46.64	53.36
1980	489	133	622	28.90	49.72	21.38	46.24	53.76
1981	536	163	699	26.74	49.94	23.32	48.29	51.71
1982	618	151	769	31.01	49.35	19.64	44.31	55.69
1983	419	141	560	24.82	50.00	25.18	50.18	49.82
1984	378	106	484	28.30	49.79	21.90	46.80	53.20
1985	448	125	573	28.40	49.78	21.82	46.71	53.29
1986	536	155	691	27.71	49.86	22.43	47.36	52.64
1987	No data collected this year							
1988	652	122	774	36.36	47.88	15.76	39.70	60.30
1989	552	146	698	29.45	49.64	20.92	45.74	54.26
1990	603	111	714	36.69	47.76	15.55	39.43	60.57

1. **Graph population changes**: Use the data in the first 3 columns of the table above to plot a line graph. This will show changes in the phenotypes: numbers of gray and white (albino) squirrels, as well as changes in the total population. Plot: **gray**, **white**, and **total** for each year:

(a) Determine by how much (as a %) total population numbers have fluctuated over the sampling period:

_____

(b) Describe the overall trend in total population numbers and any pattern that may exist:

_____
_____
_____
_____
_____
_____

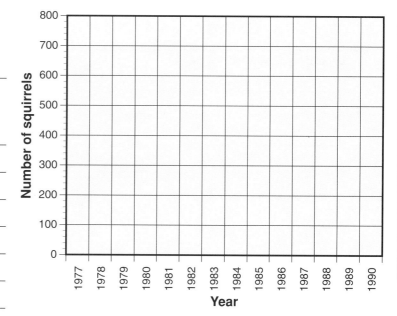

© BIOZONE International 2006-2012
ISBN: 978-1-877462-98-6
Photocopying Prohibited

The Mechanisms of Evolution

Related activities: Calculating Allele Frequencies in Populations

DA 3

2. **Graph genotype changes**: Use the data in the genotype columns of the table on the opposite page to plot a line graph. This will show changes in the allele combinations (**GG**, **Gg**, **gg**). Plot: **GG**, **Gg**, and **gg** for each year:

Describe the overall trend in the frequency of:

(a) Homozygous dominant (**GG**) genotype:

_____

_____

(b) Heterozygous (**Gg**) genotype:

_____

_____

(c) Homozygous recessive (gg) genotype:

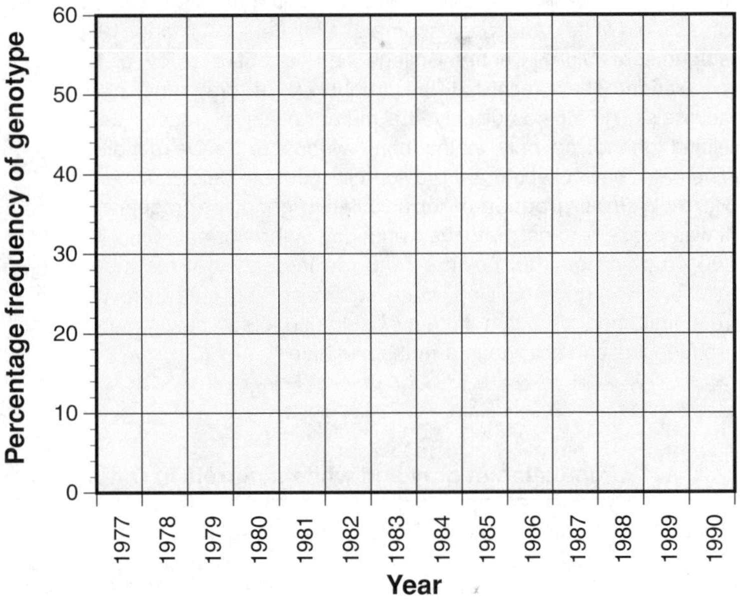

_____

_____

_____

[Graph: y-axis "Percentage frequency of genotype" 0–60; x-axis "Year" 1977–1990]

3. **Graph allele changes**: Use the data in the last two columns of the table on the previous page to plot a line graph. This will show changes in the *allele frequencies* for each of the dominant (**G**) and recessive (**g**) alleles.
Plot: the frequency of **G** and the frequency of **g**:

(a) Describe the overall trend in the frequency of the dominant allele (**G**):

_____

_____

_____

(b) Describe the overall trend in the frequency of the recessive allele (**g**):

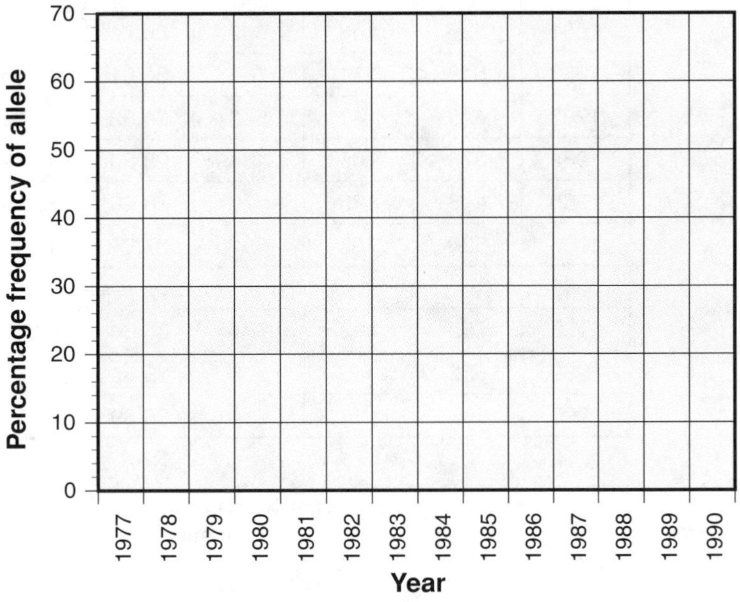

_____

_____

_____

_____

_____

[Graph: y-axis "Percentage frequency of allele" 0–70; x-axis "Year" 1977–1990]

4. (a) State which of the three graphs best indicates that a significant change may be taking place in the gene pool of this population of squirrels:

_____

(b) Give a reason for your answer: _____

_____

_____

5. Describe a possible cause of the changes in allele frequencies over the sampling period: _____

_____

_____

_____

_____

Changes in a Gene Pool

The diagram below shows an hypothetical population of beetles undergoing changes as it is subjected to two 'events'. The three phases represent a progression in time (i.e. the same gene pool, undergoing change). The beetles have two phenotypes (black and pale) determined by the amount of pigment deposited in the cuticle. The gene controlling this character is represented by two alleles **A** and **a**. Your task is to analyze the gene pool as it undergoes changes.

Phase 1: Initial gene pool

Calculate the frequencies of the allele types and allele combinations by counting the actual numbers, then working them out as percentages.

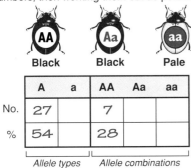

Black   Black   Pale

	A	a	AA	Aa	aa
No.	27		7		
%	54		28		

Allele types   *Allele combinations*

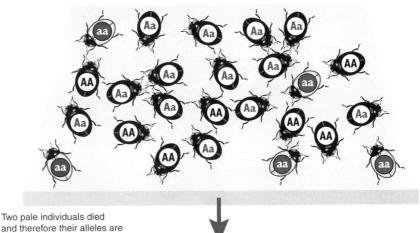

Two pale individuals died and therefore their alleles are removed from the gene pool.

Phase 2: Natural selection

In the same gene pool at a later time there was a change in the allele frequencies. This was due to the loss of certain allele combinations due to natural selection. Some of those with a genotype of aa were eliminated (poor fitness).

Calculate as for above. Do not include the individuals surrounded by small white arrows in your calculations; they are dead!

	A	a	AA	Aa	aa
No.					
%					

Phase 3: Immigration and emigration

This particular kind of beetle exhibits wandering behavior. The allele frequencies change again due to the introduction and departure of individual beetles, each carrying certain allele combinations.

Calculate as above. In your calculations, include the individual coming into the gene pool (AA), but remove the one leaving (aa).

	A	a	AA	Aa	aa
No.					
%					

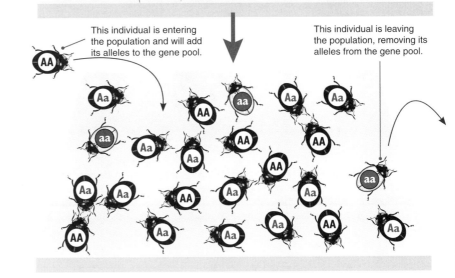

This individual is entering the population and will add its alleles to the gene pool.

This individual is leaving the population, removing its alleles from the gene pool.

1. Explain how the number of dominant alleles (A) in the genotype of a beetle affects its phenotype:

_____

_____

2. For each phase in the gene pool above (place your answers in the tables provided; some have been done for you):

    (a) Determine the relative frequencies of the two alleles: A and a. Simply total the **A** alleles and **a** alleles separately.
    (b) Determine the frequency of how the alleles come together as allele pair combinations in the gene pool (AA, Aa and aa). Count the number of each type of combination.
    (c) For each of the above, work out the frequencies as percentages:

Allele frequency = No. counted alleles ÷ Total no. of alleles x 100

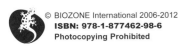
© BIOZONE International 2006-2012
ISBN: 978-1-877462-98-6
Photocopying Prohibited

Related activities: *Gene Pool Exercise, Natural Selection*
Weblinks: *Natural Selection in Populations*

PDA 3

The Mechanisms of Evolution

The Founder Effect

Occasionally, a small number of individuals from a large population may migrate away, or become isolated from, their original population. If this colonizing or 'founder' population is made up of only a few individuals, it will probably have a non-representative sample of alleles from the parent population's gene pool. As a consequence of this **founder effect**, the colonizing population may evolve differently from that of the parent population, particularly since the environmental conditions for the isolated population may be different. In some cases, it may be possible for certain alleles to be missing altogether from the individuals in the isolated population. Future generations of this population will not have this allele.

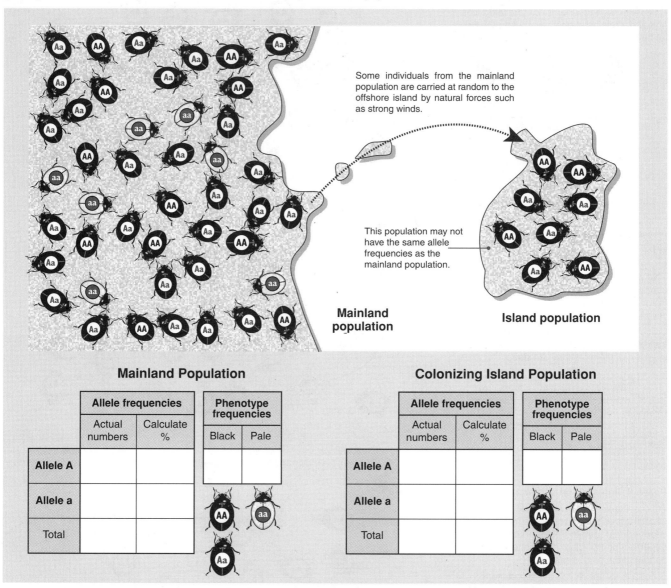

Some individuals from the mainland population are carried at random to the offshore island by natural forces such as strong winds.

This population may not have the same allele frequencies as the mainland population.

Mainland population

Island population

Mainland Population

	Allele frequencies		Phenotype frequencies	
	Actual numbers	Calculate %	Black	Pale
Allele A				
Allele a				
Total				

Colonizing Island Population

	Allele frequencies		Phenotype frequencies	
	Actual numbers	Calculate %	Black	Pale
Allele A				
Allele a				
Total				

1. Compare the mainland population to the population which ended up on the island (use the spaces in the tables above):
   (a) Count the **phenotype** numbers for the two populations (i.e. the number of black and pale beetles).
   (b) Count the **allele** numbers for the two populations: the number of dominant alleles (A) and recessive alleles (a). Calculate these as a percentage of the total number of alleles for each population.

2. How are the allele frequencies of the two populations different? _____

   _____

3. Describe some possible ways in which various types of organism can be **carried** to an offshore island:

   (a) Plants: _____

   (b) Land animals: _____

   (c) Non-marine birds: _____

4. Founder populations are usually very small. What other process may act quite rapidly to further alter allele frequencies?

   _____

   _____

© BIOZONE International 2006-2012
ISBN: 978-1-877462-98-6
Photocopying Prohibited

Related activities: Gene Pool Exercise, Genetic Drift, Oceanic Island Colonizers

Sexual Selection

The success of an individual is measured not only by the number of offspring it leaves, but also by the quality or likely reproductive success of those offspring. This means that it becomes important who its mate will be. It was Darwin (1871) who first introduced the concept of sexual selection; a special type of natural selection that produces anatomical and behavioral traits that affect an individual's ability to acquire mates. Biologists today recognize two types: **intrasexual selection** (usually male-male competition) and **intersexual selection** or mate selection. One result of either type is the evolution of **sexual dimorphism**.

Intrasexual selection

Intrasexual selection involves competition within one sex (usually males) with the winner gaining access to the opposite sex. Competition often takes place before mating, and males compete to establish dominance or secure a territory for breeding or mating. This occurs in many species of ungulates (**deer**, antelope, cattle) and in many birds. In deer and other ungulates, the males typically engage in highly ritualized battles with horns or antlers. The winners of these battles gain dominance over rival males and do most of the mating.

In other species, males compete for territories. These may contain resources or they may consist of an isolated area within a special arena used for communal courtship display (a **lek**). In lek species, males with the best territories on a lek (the dominant males) have more chances to mate with females. In some species of grouse (right), this form of sexual selection can be difficult to distinguish from intersexual selection, because once males establish their positions on the lek the females then choose among them. In species where access to females is limited and females are promiscuous, **sperm competition** may also be a feature of male-male competition.

Intersexual selection

In intersexual selection (or **mate choice**), individuals of one sex (usually the males) advertise themselves as potential mates and members of the other sex (usually the females), choose among them. Intersexual selection results in development of exaggerated ornamentation, such as elaborate plumages. Female preference for elaborate male ornaments is well supported by both anecdotal and experimental evidence. For example, in the **long-tailed widow bird** (*Euplectes progne*), females prefer males with long tails. When tails are artificially shortened or lengthened, females still prefer males with the longest tails; they therefore select for long tails, not another trait correlated with long tails.

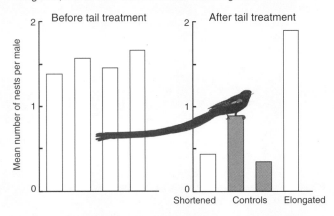

As shown above, there was no significant difference in breeding success between the groups before the tails were altered. When the tails were cut and lengthened, breeding success went down and up respectively.

In male-male competition for mates, ornamentation is used primarily to advertise superiority to rival males, and not to mortally wound opponents. However, injuries do occur, most often between closely matched rivals, where dominance must be tested and established through the aggressive use of their weaponry rather than mere ritual duels.

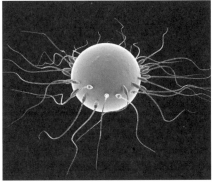

Sperm competition occurs when females remate within a relatively short space of time. The outcome of sperm competition may be determined by mating order. In some species, including those that guard their mates, the first male has the advantage, but in many the advantage accrues to the sperm of the second or subsequent males.

How do male features, such as the extravagant plumage of the peacock, persist when increasingly elaborate plumage must become detrimental to survival at some point? At first, preference for such traits must confer a survival advantage. Male adornment and female preference then advance together until a stable strategy is achieved.

1. Explain the difference between **intrasexual selection** and **mate selection**, identifying the features associated with each:

_____

_____

2. Suggest how sexual selection results in marked **sexual dimorphism**: _____

_____

_____

© BIOZONE International 2006-2012
ISBN: 978-1-877462-98-6
Photocopying Prohibited

Periodicals: Animal attraction

Related activities: Gene Pools and Evolution
Weblinks: Pheasant Sexual Selection

A 2

The Mechanisms of Evolution

The Biological Species Concept

The **species** is the basic unit of taxonomy. A **biological species** is defined as a group of organisms capable of interbreeding to produce fertile offspring. However, there are some difficulties in applying the biological species concept (BSC) in practice. Morphologically identical but reproductively isolated cryptic species and closely related species that interbreed to produce fertile hybrids (e.g. *Canis* species), indicate that the boundaries of a species gene pool can be unclear. The BSC is also more successfully applied to animals than to plants. Plants hybridize easily and can reproduce vegetatively. For some, e.g. cotton and rice, F_1 hybrids are fertile but hybrid breakdown in subsequent generations stops hybrids proliferating and maintains the parental types in the wild. In addition, the BSC cannot be applied to asexually reproducing or extinct organisms. Increasingly, biologists are using DNA analyses to clarify relationships between the related populations that we regard as one species.

Distribution of *Canis* species

The global distribution of most species of *Canis* (dogs and wolves) is shown on the map, right. The gray wolf inhabits the forests of North America, northern Europe, and Siberia. The red wolf and Mexican wolf (original distributions shown) were once distributed more widely, but are now extinct in the wild except for reintroductions. In contrast, the coyote has expanded its original range and is now found throughout North and Central America. The range of the three jackal species overlap in the open savannah of eastern Africa. The dingo is distributed throughout the Australian continent. Distribution of the domesticated dog is global as a result of the spread of human culture. The dog has been able to interbreed with all other members of the genus listed here to form fertile hybrids. Contrast this with members of the horse family, in which hybrid offspring are viable but sterile.

Interbreeding between *Canis* species

The *Canis* species illustrate problems with the traditional species concept. The domesticated dog is able to breed with other members of the same genus to produce fertile hybrids. Red wolves, gray wolves, Mexican wolves, and coyotes are all capable of interbreeding to produce fertile hybrids. Red wolves are very rare, and it is possible that hybridization with coyotes has been a factor in their decline. By contrast, the ranges of the three distinct species of jackal overlap in the Serengeti of eastern Africa. These animals are highly territorial, but simply ignore members of the other jackal species and no interbreeding takes place.

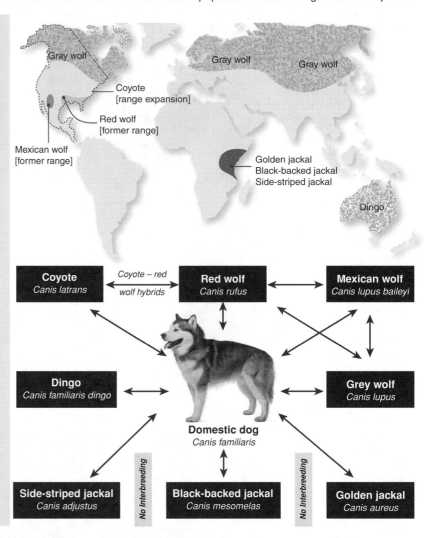

1. Describe the type of barrier that prevents the three species of jackal from interbreeding: _____

_____

2. Describe the factor that has prevented the dingo from interbreeding with other *Canis* species (apart from the dog):

_____

3. Describe a possible contributing factor to the occurrence of interbreeding between the coyote and red wolf:

_____

4. The gray wolf is a widely distributed species. Explain why the North American population is considered to be part of the same species as the northern European and Siberian populations:

_____

_____

5. Explain some of the limitations of using the biological species concept to assign species: _____

_____

_____

Related activities: The Phylogenetic Species Concept
Weblinks: The Species Concept

Periodicals: *Species and species formation*

© BIOZONE International 2006-2012
ISBN: 978-1-877462-98-6
Photocopying Prohibited

Are Ring Species Real?

A **ring species** is a connected series of closely related populations, distributed around a geographical barrier, in which the adjacent populations in the ring are able to interbreed, but those at the extremes of the ring are reproductively isolated. The ring species concept was proposed by Ernst Mayr in 1942 to account for the circum-polar distribution of species of herring gulls (*Larus* species). The idea of a ring species is attractive to biologists because it appears to show speciation in action (i.e. incipient species). However, such examples are rare, and rigorous analysis of supposed ring species, such as the herring gull complex, have shown that they do not meet all the necessary criteria to be ring species as defined. Although ring species are rare, the concept is still helpful because it can allow us to reconstruct the divergence of populations from an ancestral species. Ring species also provide evidence that speciation can occur without complete geographic isolation.

What is a Ring Species?

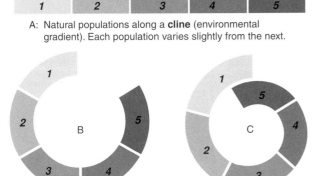

A: Natural populations along a **cline** (environmental gradient). Each population varies slightly from the next.

The variation in populations may occur in a geographical ring, e.g. around a continental shoreline (B). Adjacent populations in the cline can interbreed. If the ring closes (C), the populations at the extremes of the ring may meet but are too different to interbreed.

Criteria for a Ring Species

▶ Ring species develop from a single ancestral population with isolation by distance.

▶ They show expansion of their range around a geographic barrier, such a mountain range or desert.

▶ Adjacent populations can interbreed and are fertile (gene flow). Fertility declines with distance, and the terminal populations are not fertile (no gene flow).

The circumpolar distribution of *Larus* subspecies (still often cited in many texts) inspired Mayr to propose the ring species hypothesis. However, mtDNA studies (Liebers *et al.* 2004) have indicated that there were two ancestral gull populations (not one) and most of Mayr's subspecies actually deserve full species status. What is more, the *Larus* complex includes several species, excluded by Mayr, whose taxonomy is unclear. Ring species do appear to be a very rare phenomenon if they exist at all. In contrast, cryptic (hidden) species, which are morphologically identical but behave as (reproductively isolated) true species, appear to be quite common.

The herring gull (front) and black-backed gull (rear) do not interbreed at the ends of the circumpolar ring where they coexist. However, genetic analyses do not support a ring species.

Populations of *Ensatina* in the USA occupy a ring around California's Central Valley. While they show some of the characteristics of ring species, many of the adjacent populations are in fact genetically isolated and do not interbreed. What is more, the yellow-eyed *Ensatina* (above) has evolved to be a mimic of the toxic California newt, and this has probably driven its genetic isolation from adjacent *Ensatina* populations.

Greenish warbler populations occupy a ring around the Tibetan Plateau. Eastern and western populations meet in Siberia but do not interbreed. Analyses support them being a ring species.

1. Why is the phenomenon of ring species interesting to evolutionary biologists: _____

2. Discuss how modern genetic analyses are changing the way we view species and determine species status: _____

3. What implications might the existence of ring species have for conservation: _____

© BIOZONE International 2006-2012
ISBN: 978-1-877462-98-6
Photocopying Prohibited

Related activities: The Biological Species Concept

A 3

Ensatina in North America: Ring Species or Cryptic Species?

Ensatina eschscholtzii is a species of lungless salamander found throughout the Pacific North-West of the USA to Baja California in Mexico. *E. eschscholtzii* has long been considered a ring species, which probably expanded southwards from an ancestral population in Oregon along either side of California's Central Valley. However, molecular analyses are now indicating that the story of *Ensatina* is more complicated than first supposed. Geographically adjacent populations within the ring may be genetically isolated or comprise morphologically identical but genetically distinct **cryptic species**. Regardless of the conclusions drawn from the evidence (below), species such as *E. eschscholtzii* give us reason to reevaluate how we define species and quantify biodiversity.

Oregon Ensatina,
E. e. oregonensis

The ancestral Oregon population spread south either side of California's Central Valley. Coastal and inland populations diverged.

Oregon

Inland populations occupy the Sierra Nevada range. This inland flank of the distribution is not geographically continuous (note the gap in the ring) and most of the *Ensatina* 'subspecies' are genetically isolated from geographically adjacent 'subspecies'. In addition, the inland populations include two (or more) morphologically undistinguishable 'cryptic' species.

Painted Ensatina,
E. e. picta

Central Valley

of California

Sierra Nevada,
E. e. platensis

Yellow-eyed,
E. e. xanthoptica

Yellow blotched,
E. e. croceater

The yellow-eyed *Ensatina* has crossed the central valley to overlap in a narrow contact zone with the Sierra Nevada form. They occasionally interbreed to produce fertile offspring, but mostly the populations remain distinct.

Gap in the ring
(Mojave desert)

Monterey Ensatina,
E. e. eschscholtzii

	Criteria for a ring species	Ensatina?
1	Range expansion around both sides of an area of inhospitable habitat.	Yes
2	Lack of gene flow at the terminus of the ring.	Yes
3	Continued gene flow around the rest of the ring.	Not entirely

In southern California, the ranges of the coastal Monterey form and the inland large-blotched form overlap, but little or no gene flow occurs between them. If they interbreed, the hybrids are infertile or have extremely reduced fitness. Electrophoretic analysis of enzymes and DNA indicate that they are different species.

Large blotched,
E. e. klauberi

4. The *Ensatina* species complex fulfils two of the three criteria necessary to define a ring species (table, above left) yet does not fit comfortably with Mayr's definition of a biological species. Describe the aspects of *Ensatina* that:

   (a) Supports the idea that they are a single species: _____

   _____

   (b) Does not agree with the standard definition of a biological species: _____

   _____

5. Yellow-eyed *Ensatina* is a mimic of the toxic California newt. What might this suggest about the selection pressures on this subspecies and their influence on the rate at which the population becomes genetically distinct?

   _____

   _____

   _____

Ring Species: The Greenish Warbler

Greenish warblers (*Phylloscopus trochiloides*) are found in forests across much of northern and central Asia. They inhabit the ring of mountains surrounding the large area of desert which includes the Tibetan Plateau, and Taklamakan and Gobi deserts,

and extends into Siberia. In Siberia, two distinct subspecies coexist and do not interbreed, but are apparently connected by gene flow around the Himalayas to the south. The greenish warblers may thus form a rare example of a ring species.

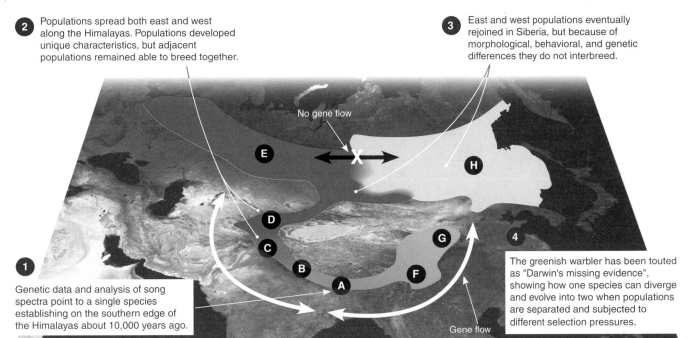

2 Populations spread both east and west along the Himalayas. Populations developed unique characteristics, but adjacent populations remained able to breed together.

3 East and west populations eventually rejoined in Siberia, but because of morphological, behavioral, and genetic differences they do not interbreed.

No gene flow

1 Genetic data and analysis of song spectra point to a single species establishing on the southern edge of the Himalayas about 10,000 years ago.

Gene flow

4 The greenish warbler has been touted as "Darwin's missing evidence", showing how one species can diverge and evolve into two when populations are separated and subjected to different selection pressures.

Song Spectra of the Greenish Warbler

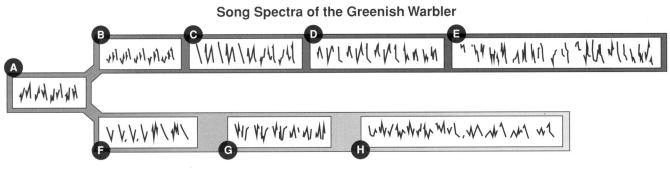

The two coexisting subspecies of greenish warblers can be distinguished by their songs and the number of bars on the wings. The warbler in western Siberia has one light bar across the top of the wing, while the warbler in eastern Siberia has two. Analysis of the songs around the ring show that all songs can be traced to the population labeled A above. Songs become progressively different moving east or west around the ring. The songs of the eastern warblers (E) and western warblers (H) in Siberia are so different that neither recognizes the other. Eastern and western forms have **subspecies status**.

JM Garg, Wikipedia CC 3.0

1. How do the eastern and western Siberian populations of greenish warblers differ? _____

_____

2. Explain how these differences occurred: _____

_____

_____

3. Explain why the greenish warbler has been touted as "evolution in action": _____

_____

_____

Related activities: Are Ring Species Real?

A 2

The Mechanisms of Evolution

The Phylogenetic Species Concept

Although the biological species concept is useful, there are many situations in which it is difficult to apply, e.g. for asexual populations, (including bacteria) or extinct organisms. In such situations, the phylogenetic species concept (PSC) can be more useful. It not reliant on the criterion of successful interbreeding and can be applied to asexually or sexually reproducing organisms, and to extinct organisms. Phylogenetic species are defined on the basis of their shared evolutionary ancestry, which is determined on the basis of **shared derived characteristics**, which may be morphological, especially for higher taxonomic

ranks, or biochemical (e.g. DNA differences). The PSC defines a species as the smallest group that all share a derived character state. It is widely applicable in palaeontology because biologists can compare both living and extinct organisms. While the phylogenetic species concept solves some difficulties, it creates others. It does not apply well to morphologically different species that are connected by gene flow. Similarly, the ability to distinguish genetically distinct but morphologically identical cryptic species on the basis of DNA analyses can lead to a proliferation of extant species that is not helpful in establishing a phylogeny.

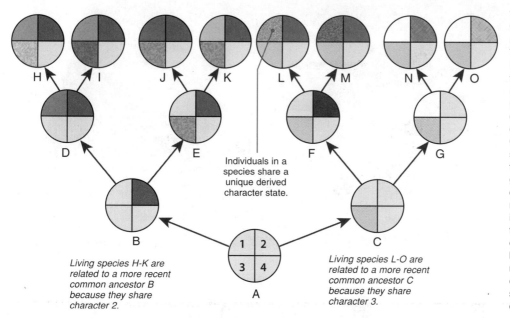

Individuals in a species share a unique derived character state.

Living species H-K are related to a more recent common ancestor B because they share character 2.

A

Living species L-O are related to a more recent common ancestor C because they share character 3.

This simplified phylogenetic tree traces four characters among 15 species (8 present and 7 ancestral). The 8 modern species (species H-O) share a character (4) derived from a distant common ancestor (A). Although the primitive character unites all 8 species, the branching of the tree is based on characters derived from the ancestral ones. Classification on the basis of shared derived characters defines the species as the smallest group diagnosable by a unique combination of characters. If large numbers of characters are included in the analysis, it is easy to see how this method results in a proliferation of species that may or may not be meaningful. Under the PSC model, there are no subspecies; either a population is a phylogenetic species or it is not taxonomically distinguishable.

Tree sparrows (*P. montanus*) are ~10% smaller than the similar house sparrow but the two species hybridize freely.

House sparrows (*P. domesticus*) are widespread with many intermediate "subspecies" of unknown status.

Mallards are infamous for their ability to hybridize freely with a large number of other duck "species".

True sparrows all belong to the genus *Passer*. There are a large number of species distinguished on the basis of song, plumage, and size. A vestigial dorsal outer primary feather and an extra bone in the tongue are ancestral characters. Many populations are not good biological species in that they hybridize freely to produce fertile offspring. A similar situation exists within the genus *Anas* of dabbling ducks (which includes the mallards). Many birds are best described using the PSC rather than the BSC.

1. (a) Explain the basis by which species are assigned under the PSC: _____

    _____

    _____

    (b) Describe one problem with the use of the PSC: _____

    _____

    (c) Describe situations where the use of the PSC might be more appropriate than the BSC: _____

    _____

    _____

2. Suggest how genetic techniques could be used to elucidate the phylogeny of a cluster of related phylogenetic species:

    _____

    _____

Related activities: Isolating Mechanisms

Weblinks: The Species Concept

Periodicals:

What is a species?

© BIOZONE International 2006-2012
ISBN: 978-1-877462-98-6
Photocopying Prohibited

Isolation and Species Formation

Isolating mechanisms are barriers to successful interbreeding between species. Reproductive isolation is fundamental to the **biological species concept**, which defines a species by its inability to breed with other species to produce fertile offspring. Prezygotic isolating mechanisms act before fertilization occurs, preventing species ever mating, whereas postzygotic barriers take effect after fertilization. **Geographical barriers** are not regarded as reproductive isolating mechanisms because they are not part of the species' biology, although they are often a necessary precursor to reproductive isolation in sexually reproducing populations. Ecological isolating mechanisms are those that isolate gene pools on the basis of ecological preferences, e.g habitat selection. Although ecological and geographical isolation are sometimes confused, they are quite distinct, as ecological isolation involves a component of the species biology. Similarly, the **temporal isolation** of species, through differences in the timing of important life cycle events, effectively prevents potentially interbreeding species from successfully reproducing.

Geographical Isolation

Geographical isolation describes the isolation of a species population (gene pool) by some kind of physical barrier, for example, mountain range, water body, isthmus, desert, or ice sheet. Geographical isolation is a frequent first step in the subsequent reproductive isolation of a species. For example, geological changes to the lake basins has been instrumental in the subsequent proliferation of cichlid fish species in the rift lakes of East Africa (right). Similarly, many Galápagos Island species (e.g. iguanas, finches) are now quite distinct from the Central and South American species from which they arose after isolation from the mainland.

Ecological (Habitat) Isolation

Ecological isolation describes the existence of a **prezygotic reproductive barrier** between two species (or sub-species) as a result of them occupying or breeding in different habitats within the same general geographical area. Ecological isolation includes small scale differences (e.g. ground or tree dwelling) and broad differences (e.g. desert vs grasslands). The red-browed and brown **treecreepers** (*Climacteris* spp.) are sympatric in south-eastern Australia and both species feed largely on ants. However the brown spends most of its time foraging on the ground or on fallen logs while the red-browed forages almost entirely in the trees.

Ecological isolation often follows geographical isolation, but in many cases the geographical barriers may remain in part. For example, five species of **antelope squirrels** occupy different habitat ranges throughout the southwestern United States and northern Mexico, a region divided in part by the Grand Canyon. The white tailed antelope squirrel is widely distributed in desert areas to the north and south of the canyon, while the smaller, more specialized Harris' antelope squirrel has a much more limited range only to the south in southern Arizona. The Grand Canyon still functions as a barrier to dispersal but the species are now ecologically isolated as well.

Geographical and Ecological Isolation of Species

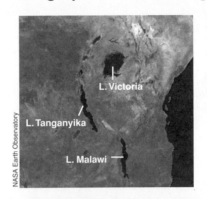
L. Victoria
L. Tanganyika
L. Malawi
NASA Earth Observatory

Malawi cichlid species
istock

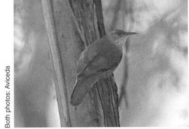
Both photos: Aviceda
Red-browed treecreeper

Brown treecreeper

UtahCamera
White-tailed antelope squirrel

istock
The Grand Canyon - a massive rift in the Colorado Plateau

Photo: Allan and Elaine Wilson
Harris' antelope squirrel

1. Describe the role of isolating mechanisms in maintaining the integrity of a species: _____

_____

_____

2. (a) Why is geographical isolation not regarded as a reproductive isolating mechanism? _____

_____

(b) Explain why, despite this, it often precedes reproductive isolation: _____

_____

3. Distinguish between geographical and ecological isolation: _____

_____

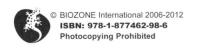
© BIOZONE International 2006-2012
ISBN: 978-1-877462-98-6
Photocopying Prohibited

Periodicals: Cichlids of the Rift Lakes

Related activities: Reproductive Isolation, Speciation in Australia

A 2

The Mechanisms of Evolution

Reproductive Isolation

Reproductive isolation prevents interbreeding (and therefore gene flow) between species. Any factor that impedes two species from producing viable, fertile hybrids contributes to reproductive isolation. Single barriers may not completely stop gene flow, so most species commonly have more than one type of barrier.

Single barriers to reproduction (including geographical barriers) often precede the development of a suite of reproductive isolating mechanisms (RIMs). Most operate before fertilization (prezygotic RIMs) with postzyotic RIMs being important in preventing offspring between closely related species.

Temporal Isolation

Individuals from different species do not mate because they are active during different times of the day, or in different seasons. Plants flower at different times of the year or even at different times of the day to avoid hybridization (e.g. the orchid genus *Dendrobium*, which occupy the same location and flower on different days). Closely related animal species may have quite different breeding seasons or periods of emergence. **Periodical cicadas** (right) of the genus *Magicicada* are so named because members of each species in a particular region are developmentally synchronized, despite very long life cycles. Once their underground period of development (13 or 17 years depending on the species) is over, the entire population emerges at much the same time to breed.

Gamete Isolation

The gametes from different species are often incompatible, so even if they meet they do not survive. For animals where fertilization is internal, the sperm may not survive in the reproductive tract of another species. If the sperm does survive and reach the ovum, chemical differences in the gametes prevent fertilization. Gamete isolation is particularly important in aquatic environments where the gametes are released into the water and fertilized externally, such as in reproduction in frogs. Chemical recognition is also used by flowering plants to recognize pollen from the same species.

Behavioral (ethological) Isolation

Behavioral isolation operates through differences in species courtship behaviors. Courtship is a necessary prelude to mating in many species and courtship behaviors are species specific. Mates of the same species are attracted with distinctive, usually ritualized, dances, vocalizations, and body language. Because they are not easily misinterpreted, the courtship behaviors of one species will be unrecognized and ignored by individuals of another species. Birds exhibit a remarkable range of courtship displays. The use of song is widespread but ritualized movements, including nest building, are also common. For example, the elaborate courtship bowers of bowerbirds are well known, and Galápagos frigatebirds have an elaborate display in which they inflate a bright red gular pouch (right). Amongst insects, empid flies have some of the most elaborate of courtship displays. They are aggressive hunters so ritualized behavior involving presentation of a prey item facilitates mating. The sexual organs of the flies are also like a lock-and-key, providing mechanical reproductive isolation as well (see below).

Mechanical (morphological) Isolation

Structural differences (incompatibility) in the anatomy of reproductive organs prevents sperm transfer between individuals of different species. This is an important isolating mechanism preventing breeding between closely related species of arthropods. Many flowering plants have coevolved with their animal pollinators and have flowers structures to allow only that insect access. Structural differences in the flowers and pollen of different plant species prevents cross breeding because pollen transfer is restricted to specific pollinators and the pollen itself must be species compatible.

Prezygotic Isolating Mechanisms

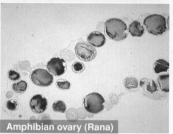
Amphibian ovary (Rana)

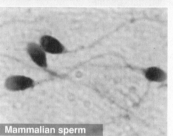
Mammalian sperm

Male frigatebird courtship display

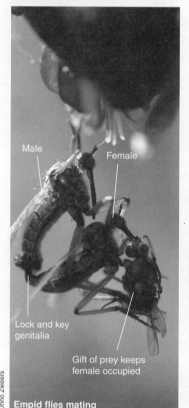
Male
Female
Lock and key genitalia
Gift of prey keeps female occupied
Empid flies mating

Male tree frog calling

Wing beating in male sage grouse

Damselflies mating

Complex flowers in orchids

Related activities: Isolation and Species Formation

Periodicals:
Listen, we're different

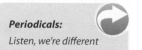

© BIOZONE International 2006-2012
ISBN: 978-1-877462-98-6
Photocopying Prohibited

KEY TERMS: Flash Card Game

The cards below have a keyword or term printed on one side and its definition printed on the opposite side. The aim is to win as many cards as possible from the table. To play the game.....

1) Cut out the cards and lay them definition side down on the desk. You will need one set of cards between two students.

2) Taking turns, choose a card and, BEFORE you pick it up, state

your own best definition of the keyword to your opponent.

3) Check the definition on the opposite side of the card. If both you and your opponent agree that your stated definition matches, then keep the card. If your definition does not match then return the card to the desk.

4) Once your turn is over, your opponent may choose a card.

Allele frequency	Selection pressure	Ring species
Reproductive isolation	Allopatric (allopatry)	Genetic drift
Natural selection	Genetic equilibrium	Mutation
Heterozygous advantage	Speciation	Founder effect

The Mechanisms of Evolution

R 2

When you've finished the game keep these cutouts and use them as flash cards!

A population sharing the same gene pool where groups next to each other are able to interbreed but groups at the extreme ends of the population can not.

Those factors that collectively influence the direction of natural selection.

The number of times an allele appears in a population.

Random changes in allele frequency as a result of sampling error. An important evolutionary phenomenon in small populations.

A term for physically separated populations. In reference to speciation, a term to mean speciation in which the populations are physically separated.

The situation in which members of a group of organisms breed with each other but not with members of other groups.

A change in the base sequence of DNA; the ultimate source of new alleles.

The condition in which there is no change in allele frequencies from generation to generation (i.e. no evolution).

The process by which traits become more or less common in a population through differential survival and reproduction.

The loss of genetic variation occurring when a new population is established by a small number of individuals from a larger population.

The division of one species, during evolution, into two or more separate species.

The situation in population genetics in which the heterozygous condition has higher fitness than either of the homozygous conditions.

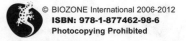

Patterns of Evolution

Key concepts

▶ Larger scale patterns of evolution involve the diversification and extinction of species.

▶ Divergent evolution is often associated with the diversification of species into new niches.

▶ Adaptive radiation and subsequent sympatry are associated with character displacement.

▶ Evolutionary developmental biology provides a explanation for the diversity of organisms and the rapid evolution of novel forms.

Key terms

adaptive radiation

analogous structures (homoplasies)

background extinction rate

coevolution

common ancestor

convergent evolution

divergent evolution (=cladogenesis)

evo-devo

extinction

homologous structures (homologies)

homoplasies

mass extinction

monophyletic

parallel evolution

phyletic gradualism (=anagenesis)

phylogeny

punctuated equilibrium

sequential evolution

Objectives

☐ 1. Use the **KEY TERMS** to help you understand and complete these objectives.

Patterns of Evolution   pages 25-26, 82-105

☐ 2. Using examples, describe patterns of species formation: **sequential evolution** (also known as anagenesis), **divergent evolution** (also known as cladogenesis), **coevolution**, and **adaptive radiation**.

☐ 3. Explain how evolutionary change over time has resulted in a great diversity among living organisms.

☐ 4. Describe and explain **convergent evolution**.

☐ 5. Explain how **analogous structures** (analogies) may arise as a result of convergence. Distinguish between **analogies** and **homologies** and explain the role of homology in identifying evolutionary relationships.

☐ 6. Describe examples of **coevolution**, including in flowering plants and their pollinators, parasites and their hosts, and predators and their prey (including herbivory). Discuss the evidence for coevolution in species with close ecological relationships.

☐ 7. Understand that some biologists also recognise **parallel evolution** to indicate evolution along similar lines in related groups.

☐ 8. Distinguish between the **punctuated equilibrium** and **phyletic gradualism** (gradualism) models for the pace of evolutionary change. Discuss the evidence for each model and discuss the evidence for each in different taxa.

☐ 9. Describe the role of **extinction** in evolution. Distinguish clearly between **background extinction rates** and **mass extinction**. Identify the major **mass extinctions** and discuss the theories for their causes.

☐ 10. Describe examples of evolution (including speciation). As appropriate, include reference to important features of the species divergence:
   • Geographical barriers between populations.
   • Habitat range and niche differentiation.
   • Any zones of overlap in distribution (sympatry).
   • Recent range expansions.

☐ 11. Recall how **evolutionary developmental biology** is providing valuable evidence for the mechanisms of evolution and the origin of novel forms.

Classification and Phylogeny   pages 91-96, 103

☐ 12. Explain how classification systems (should) reflect the evolutionary relationships and history (**phylogeny**) of organisms. To illustrate this, describe the evolution and classification of a taxonomic group, e.g. mammals, ratites, parrots, New Zealand *Hebe*.

Periodicals:
Listings for this chapter are on page 122

Weblinks:
www.thebiozone.com/weblink/Evol-2986.html

Presentation Media
EVOLUTION:
Evolution

Small Flies and Giant Buttercups

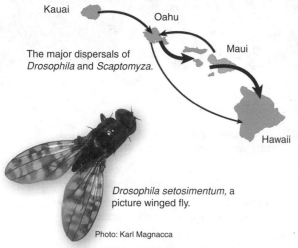

The major dispersals of *Drosophila* and *Scaptomyza*.

Drosophila setosimentum, a picture winged fly.

Photo: Karl Magnacca

Photo: Velela

Drosophilidae (commonly known as fruit flies) are a group of small flies found almost everywhere in the world. Two genera, *Drosophila* and *Scaptomyza* are found in the Hawaiian islands and between them there are more than 800 species present on a land area of just 16,500 km^2; it is one of the densest concentrations of related species found anywhere. The flies range from 1.5 mm to 20 mm in length and display a startling range of wing forms and patterns, body shapes and colors, and head and leg shapes. This diverse array of species and characteristics has made these flies the subject of much evolutionary and genetics research. Genetic analyses show that they are all related to a single species that may have arrived on the islands around 8 million years ago and diversified to exploit a range of unoccupied niches. Older species appear on the older islands and more recent species appear as one moves from the oldest to the newest islands. Such evidence points to numerous colonisation events as new islands emerged from the sea. The volcanic nature of the islands means that newly isolated environments are a frequent occurrence. For example, forested areas may become divided by lava flows, so that flies in one region diverge rapidly from flies in another just tens of metres away. One such species is *D. silvestris*. Males have a series of hairs on their forelegs, which they brush against females during courtship. Males in the northeastern part of the island have many more of these hairs than the males on the southwestern side of the island. While still the same species, the two demes are already displaying structural and behavioural isolation. Behavioural isolation is clearly an important phenomenon in drosophilid speciation. A second species, *D. heteroneura*, is closely related to *D. silvestris* and the two species live sympatrically. Although hybrid offspring are fully viable, hybridization rarely occurs because male courtship displays are very different.

New Zealand alpine buttercups (*Ranunculus*) are some of the largest in the world and are also the product of repeated speciation events. There are 14 species of *Ranunculus* in New Zealand; more than in the whole of North and South America combined. They occupy five distinct habitats ranging from snowfields and scree slopes to bogs. Genetic studies have shown that this diversity is the result of numerous isolation events following the growth and recession of glaciers. As the glaciers retreat, alpine habitat becomes restricted and populations are isolated at the tops of mountains. This restricts gene flow and provides the environment for species divergence. When the glaciers expand again, the extent of the alpine habitat increases, allowing isolated populations to come in contact and closely related species to hybridize.

1. Explain why so many drosophilidae are present in Hawaii: _____

_____

_____

_____

2. Explain why these flies are of interest: _____

_____

_____

3. Describe the relationship between the age of the islands and the age of the fly species: _____

_____

_____

_____

4. Explain why New Zealand has so many alpine buttercups: _____

_____

_____

_____

_____

_____

_____

Related activities: Allopatric Speciation

© BIOZONE International 2006-2012
ISBN: 978-1-877462-98-6
Photocopying Prohibited

Convergent Evolution

Not all similarities between species are the result of common ancestry. Species from different evolutionary lineages may come to resemble each other if they have similar ecological roles and natural selection has shaped similar adaptations. This is called **convergent evolution** or **convergence**. It can be difficult to distinguish convergent and parallel evolution, as both produce similarity of form. The distinction is somewhat arbitrary and relates to how recently the taxa shared a common ancestor. Generally, similarity of form arising in closely related lineages (e.g. within marsupial mice) is regarded as parallelism, whereas similarity arising in more distantly related taxa is convergence (e.g. similarities between marsupial mice and placental mice).

Convergence in Swimming Form

Selection pressures to solve similar problems in particular environments may result in similarity of form and function in unrelated species. The development of succulent forms in unrelated plant groups (*Euphorbia* and the cactus family) is an example of **convergence** in plants. In the example (right), the selection pressures of the aquatic environment have produced a similar **streamlined** body shape in unrelated vertebrate groups. Icthyosaurs, penguins, and dolphins each evolved from terrestrial species that took up an aquatic lifestyle. Their general body form has evolved to become similar to that of the shark, which has always been aquatic. Structures that appear similar because of convergence are called **analogous structures** or **homoplasies**. Note that flipper shape in mammals, birds, and reptiles is a result of convergence, but its origin from the pentadactyl limb is an example of **homology**.

Analogous Structures

Analogous structures are those that have the same function and often the same appearance, but **quite different origins**. The example on the right illustrates how the **eye** has developed independently in two unrelated taxa. The appearance of the eye is similar, but there is no genetic relatedness between the two groups (mammals and cephalopod mollusks). The **wings** of birds and insects are also homoplasies. The wings have the same function, but the two taxa do not share a common ancestor. *Longisquama*, a lizard-like creature that lived about 220 mya, also had 'wings' that probably allowed gliding between trees. These 'wings' were not a modification of the forearm (as in birds), but highly modified long scales or feathers extending from its back.

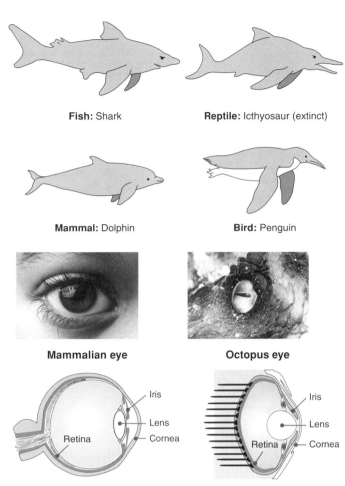

Fish: Shark

Reptile: Icthyosaur (extinct)

Mammal: Dolphin

Bird: Penguin

Mammalian eye

Octopus eye

Iris — Lens — Cornea — Retina (Mammalian eye)

Iris — Lens — Cornea — Retina (Octopus eye)

1. In the example above illustrating convergence in swimming form, describe two ways in which the body form has evolved in response to the particular selection pressures of the aquatic environment:

   (a) _____

   _____

   (b) _____

   _____

2. Describe two of the selection pressures that have influenced the body form of the swimming animals above:

   (a) _____

   (b) _____

3. When early taxonomists encountered new species in the Pacific region and the Americas, they were keen to assign them to existing taxonomic families based on their apparent similarity to European species. In recent times, many of the new species have been found to be quite unrelated to the European families they were assigned to. Explain why the traditional approach did not reveal the true evolutionary relationships of the new species:

   _____

   _____

   _____

© BIOZONE International 2006-2012
ISBN: 978-1-877462-98-6
Photocopying Prohibited

Periodicals:
Which came first?

Related activities: Adaptations and Fitness
Weblinks: Convergent Evolution

RA 2

86

4. For each of the paired examples, briefly describe the adaptations of body shape, diet and locomotion that appear to be similar in both forms, and the likely selection pressures that are acting on these mammals to produce similar body forms:

Convergence Between Marsupials and Placentals

Australia

Marsupial and **placental** mammals diverged very early in mammalian evolution (about 120 mya), probably in what is now the Americas. Marsupials were widespread throughout the ancient supercontinent of Gondwana as it began to break up through the Cretaceous, but then became isolated on the southern continents, while the placentals diversified in the Americas and elsewhere, displacing the marsupials in most habitats around the world. Australia's isolation from other landmasses in the Eocene meant that the Australian marsupials escaped competition with the placentals and diversified into a wide variety of forms, ecologically equivalent to the North American placental species.

North America

Some older sources cite this example as one of parallelism, rather than convergence. However, a greater degree of morphological difference than now once separated the ancestors of the placental and marsupial lineages being compared, making this a case of convergence, not parallelism.

Marsupial Mammals

Placental Mammals

Marsupial		Placental
Wombat	(a) Adaptations: Rodent-like teeth, eat roots and above ground plants, and can excavate burrows. Selection pressures: Diet requires chisel-like teeth for gnawing. The need to seek safety from predators on open grassland.	Woodchuck
Flying phalanger	(b) Adaptations: Selection pressures:	Flying squirrel
Marsupial mole	(c) Adaptations: Selection pressures:	Mole
Marsupial mouse	(d) Adaptations: Selection pressures:	Mouse
Tasmanian wolf (tiger)	(e) Adaptations: Selection pressures:	Wolf
Long-eared bandicoot	(f) Adaptations: Selection pressures:	Jack rabbit

© BIOZONE International 2006-2012
ISBN: 978-1-877462-98-6
Photocopying Prohibited

Coevolution

The term **coevolution** is used to describe cases where two (or more) species reciprocally affect each other's evolution. Each party in a coevolutionary relationship exerts selective pressures on the other and, over time, the species develop a relationship that may involve mutual dependency. Coevolution is a likely consequence when different species have close ecological interactions with one another. These ecological relationships include predator-prey and parasite-host relationships and mutualistic relationships such as those between plants and their pollinators. There are many examples of coevolution amongst parasites or pathogens and their hosts, and between predators and their prey, as shown on the following page.

Swollen-thorn *Acacia* lack the cyanogenic glycosides found in related Acacia spp. and the thorns are large and hollow, providing living space for the aggressive, stinging *Pseudomyrmex* ants which patrol the plant and protect it from browsing herbivores. The *Acacia* also provides the ants with protein rich food.

Photo courtesy of Alex Wild

Hummingbirds are important pollinators in the tropics. Their needle-like bills and long tongues can take nectar from flowers with deep tubes. Their ability to hover enables them to feed quickly from dangling flowers. As they feed, their heads are dusted with pollen, which is efficiently transferred between flowers.

Butterflies find flowers by vision and smell them after landing to judge their nectar source. Like bees, they can remember characteristics of desirable flowers and so exhibit constancy, which benefits both pollinator and plant. Butterfly flowers are very fragrant and are blue, purple, deep pink, red, or orange.

Bees are excellent pollinators; they are strong enough to enter intricate flowers and have medium length tongues which can collect nectar from many flower types. They have good color vision, which extends into the UV, but they are red-blind, so bee pollinated flowers are typically blue, purplish, or white and they may have nectar guides that are visible as spots.

Beetles represent a very ancient group of insects with thousands of modern species. Their high diversity has been attributed to extensive coevolution with flowering plants. Beetles consume the ovules as well as pollen and nectar and there is evidence that ovule herbivory by beetles might have driven the evolution of protective carpels in angiosperms.

NZ's short-tailed bat pollinates *Dactylanthus* flowers on the forest floor

DoC

Bats are nocturnal and color-blind but have an excellent sense of smell and are capable of long flights. Flowers that have coevolved with bat pollinators are open at night and have light or drab colors that do not attract other pollinators. Bat pollinated flowers also produce strong fragrances that mimic the smell of bats and have a wide bell shape for easy access.

1. Using examples, explain what you understand by the term coevolution: _____

_____

_____

_____

_____

2. Describe some of the strategies that have evolved in plants to attract pollinators: _____

_____

_____

_____

_____

_____

© BIOZONE International 2006-2012
ISBN: 978-1-877462-98-6
Photocopying Prohibited

Weblinks: *The Evolutionary Arms Race, The Coevolutionary Arms Race, Toxic Newts*

RA 3

Predators, Parasites, and Coevolution

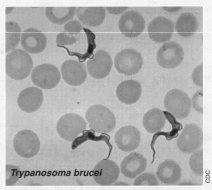
Trypanosoma brucei

Predators have obviously evolved to exploit their prey, and have evolved effective offensive weapons and hunting ability. Prey have evolved numerous strategies to protect themselves from predators, including large size and strength, protective coverings, defensive weapons, and toxicity. Lions have evolved the ability to hunt cooperatively to increase their chance of securing a kill from swift herding species such as zebra and gazelles.

Female *Helicornius* butterflies will avoid laying their eggs on plants already occupied by eggs, because their larvae are highly cannibalistic. Passionfruit plants (*Passiflora*) have exploited this by creating fake, yellow eggs on leaves and buds. *Passiflora* has many chemical defenses against herbivory, but these have been breached by *Heliconius*. It has thus counter-evolved new defenses against this herbivory by this genus.

Trypanosomes provide a good example of **host-parasite coevolution**. Trypanosomes must evolve strategies to evade their host's defenses, but their virulence is constrained by needing to keep their host alive. Molecular studies show that *Trypanosoma brucei* coevolved in Africa with the first hominids around 5 mya, but *T. cruzi* contact with human hosts occurred in South America only after settlements were made by nomadic cultures.

3. Explain how coevolution could lead to an increase in biodiversity: _____

_____

_____

_____

_____

_____

4. Discuss some of the possible consequences of species competition: _____

_____

_____

_____

_____

_____

_____

5. The analogy of an "arms race" is often used to explain the coevolution of exploitative relationships such as those of a parasite and its host. Form a small group to discuss this idea and then suggest how the analogy is flawed:

_____

_____

_____

_____

_____

_____

_____

_____

_____

Pollination Syndromes

The mutualistic relationship between plants and their pollinators represents a classic case of coevolution. Flower structure has evolved in many different ways in response to the many types of animal pollinators. Flowers and pollinators have coordinated traits known as **pollination syndromes**. This makes it relatively easy to deduce pollinators type from the appearance of flowers (and vice versa). Plants and animals involved in such pollination associations often become highly specialized in ways that improve pollination efficiency: innovation by one party leads to some response from the other.

Controlling Pollinator Access

Flowers control pollinator access by flower shape and position.

Dandelion

Rigid inflorescences offer a stable landing platform to small or heavy insects, such as bumblebees.

Fuschia

Only animals that can hover can collect rewards from and pollinate flowers that hang upside down.

Attracting Pollinators

Flowers advertise the presence of nectar and pollen, with color, scent, shape, and arrangement.

Rose

While many flowers, like roses, are fragrant, flowers pollinated by flies (right) can give off dung or rotten meat smells.

Daisy

Nectar guides help the pollinator to locate nectar and pollen. In this flower, the inner petals reflect UV.

Common Pollination Syndromes: Insects

Beetles

Ancient insect group
Good sense of smell
Hard, smooth bodies

Beetle-pollinated flowers

Ancient plant groups
Strong, fruity odours
Large, often flat, with easy access

Nectar-feeding flies

Sense nectar with feet
Tubular mouthparts

Nectar-feeding fly-pollinated flowers

Simple flowers with easy access
red or light color, little odour

Moths

Many active at night
Good sense of smell
Feed with long, narrow tongues
Some need landing platforms

Moth-pollinated flowers

Flowers may be open at night
Fragrant; with heavy, musky scent
Nectar in narrow, deep tubes
landing platforms often provided

Carrion flies

Attracted by heat, odours, or or color of carrion or dung.
Food in the form of nectar or pollen not required.

Carrion fly-pollinated flowers

Colored to resemble dung or carrion
Produce heat or foul odours
No nectar or pollen reward offered

Common Pollination Syndromes: Vertebrates

Birds

Most require a perching site
Good color vision, including red
Poor sense of smell
Feed during daylight
High energy requirements

Bird-pollinated flowers

Large and damage resistant
Often red or other bright colors
Not particularly fragrant
Open during the day
Copious nectar produced

Bats

Active at night
High food requirements
Color blind
Good sense of smell
Cannot fly in foliage
High blossom intelligence

Bat-pollinated flowers

Open at night
Plentiful nectar and pollen offered
Light or dingy colors
Strong, often bat-like odours
Open shape, easy access
Pendulous or on the trunks of trees

Non-flying mammals

Relatively large size
High energy requirements
Color vision may be lacking
Good sense of smell

Non-bat mammal-pollinated flowers

Robust, damage resistant
Copious, sugar-rich nectar
Dull colored
Odorous, but not necessarily fragrant

1. (a) Describe a common pollination syndrome of an insect: _____

(b) Describe a common pollination syndrome of a vertebrate: _____

2. Suggest how knowledge of pollination syndromes might be used to develop testable predictions about plant and animal pollination relationships:

Patterns of Evolution

© BIOZONE International 2006-2012
ISBN: 978-1-877462-98-6
Photocopying Prohibited

Related activities: Coevolution

A 2

Geographical Distribution

The camel family, Camelidae, consists of six modern-day species that have survived on three continents: Asia, Africa and South America. They are characterized by having only two functional toes, supported by expanded pads for walking on sand or snow. The slender snout bears a cleft upper lip. The recent distribution of the camel family is fragmented. Geophysical forces such as plate tectonics and the ice age cycles have controlled the extent of their distribution. South America, for example, was separated from North America until the end of the Pliocene, about 2 million years ago. Three general principles about the dispersal and distribution of land animals are:

- When very closely related animals (as shown by their anatomy) were present at the same time in widely separated parts of the world, it is highly probable that there was no barrier to their movement in one or both directions between the localities in the past.
- The most effective barrier to the movement of land animals (particularly mammals) was a sea between continents (as was caused by changing sea levels during the ice ages).
- The scattered distribution of modern species may be explained by the movement out of the area they originally occupied, or extinction in those regions between modern species.

Origin and Dispersal of the Camel Family

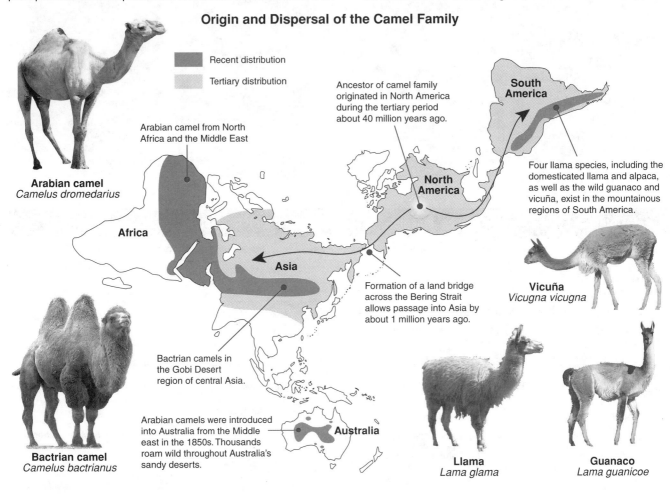

Recent distribution

Tertiary distribution

Ancestor of camel family originated in North America during the tertiary period about 40 million years ago.

Arabian camel from North Africa and the Middle East

Arabian camel
Camelus dromedarius

Africa

Asia

North America

South America

Four llama species, including the domesticated llama and alpaca, as well as the wild guanaco and vicuña, exist in the mountainous regions of South America.

Formation of a land bridge across the Bering Strait allows passage into Asia by about 1 million years ago.

Bactrian camels in the Gobi Desert region of central Asia.

Bactrian camel
Camelus bactrianus

Arabian camels were introduced into Australia from the Middle east in the 1850s. Thousands roam wild throughout Australia's sandy deserts.

Australia

Vicuña
Vicugna vicugna

Llama
Lama glama

Guanaco
Lama guanicoe

1. The early camel ancestors were able to move into the tropical regions of Central and South America. Explain why this did not happen in southern Asia and southern Africa:

2. Arabian camels are found wild in the Australian outback. Explain how they got there and why they were absent during prehistoric times:

3. The camel family originated in North America. Explain why there are no camels in North America now:

4. Suggest how early camels managed to get to Asia from North America:

5. Describe the present distribution of the camel family and explain why it is scattered (discontinuous):

© BIOZONE International 2006-2012
ISBN: 978-1-877462-98-6
Photocopying Prohibited

Adaptive Radiation in Mammals

Adaptive radiation is diversification (both structural and ecological) among the descendants of a single ancestral group to occupy different niches. The mammals underwent a spectacular adaptive radiation immediately following the sudden extinction of the non-avian dinosaurs. Most of the modern mammalian taxa became established very early. The diagram below shows the divergence of the mammals into major orders; many occupying niches left vacant by the dinosaurs. The vertical extent of each grey shape shows the time span for which that particular mammal order has existed (note that the scale for the geological time scale in the diagram is not linear). Those that reach the top of the chart have survived to the present day. The width of a gray shape indicates how many species were in existence at any given time (narrow means there were few, wide means there were many). The dotted lines indicate possible links between the various mammal orders for which there is no direct fossil evidence.

Patterns of Evolution

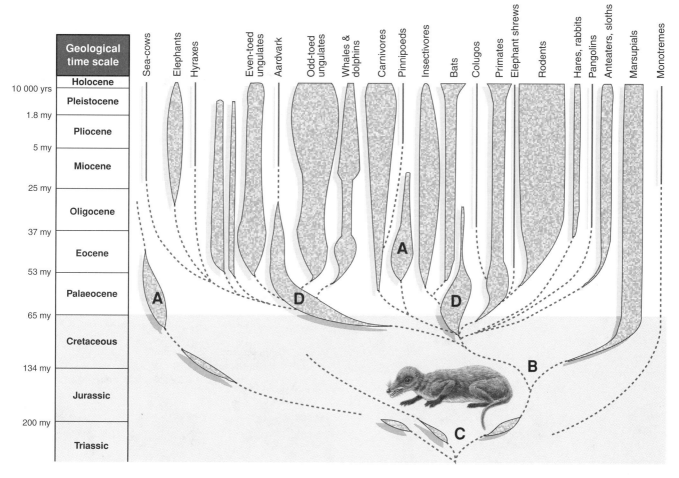

1. In general terms, discuss the **adaptive radiation** that occurred in mammals: _____

   _____

   _____

2. Name the term that you would use to describe the animal groups at point **C** (above): _____

3. Explain what occurred at point **B** (above): _____

   _____

4. Describe two things that the animal orders labelled **D** (above) have in common:

   (a) _____

   (b) _____

5. Identify the two orders that appear to have been most successful in terms of the number of species produced:

   _____

6. Explain what has happened to the mammal orders labelled **A** in the diagram above: _____

   _____

7. Identify the **epoch** during which there was the most adaptive radiation: _____

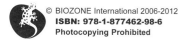
© BIOZONE International 2006-2012
ISBN: 978-1-877462-98-6
Photocopying Prohibited

Periodicals:
The rise of mammals

Related activities: *Patterns of Evolution*
Weblinks: *Homologous Structures*

RDA 3

8. Describe two key features that distinguish mammals from other vertebrates:

(a) ______________________ (b) ______________________

9. Describe the principal reproductive features that distinguish each of the major mammalian lines (sub-classes):

(a) Monotremes: ______________________

(b) Marsupials: ______________________

(c) Placentals: ______________________

10. There are 18 orders of placental mammals (or 17 in schemes that include the pinnipeds within the Carnivora). Their names and a brief description of the type of mammal belonging to each group is provided below. Identify and label each of the diagrams with the correct name of their Order:

Orders of Placental Mammals

Order	Description
Insectivora	Insect-eating mammals
Macroscelidae	Elephant shrews (formerly classified with insectivores)
Chiroptera	Bats
Cetacea	Whales and dolphins
Pholidota	Pangolins
Rodentia	Rodents
Probiscidea	Elephants
Sirenia	Sea-cows (manatees)
Artiodactyla	Even-toed hoofed mammals
Dermoptera	Colugos
Primates	Primates
Xenarthra	Anteaters, sloths, and armadillos
Lagomorpha	Pikas, hares, and rabbits
Carnivora	Flesh-eating mammals (canids, rac coons, bears, cats)
Pinnipedia	Seals, sealions, walruses. (Often now included as a sub-order of Carnivora).
Tubulidentata	Aardvark
Hyracoidea	Hyraxes
Perissodactyla	Odd-toed hoofed mammals

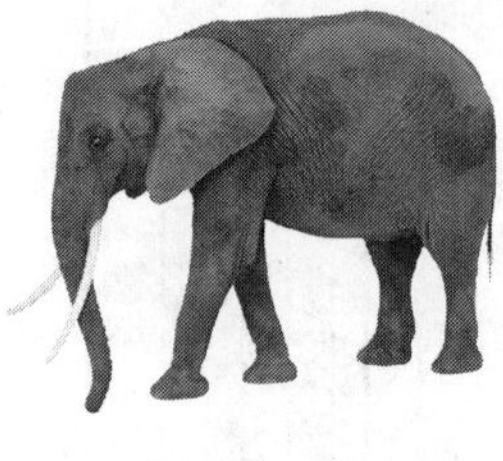
1 ______________

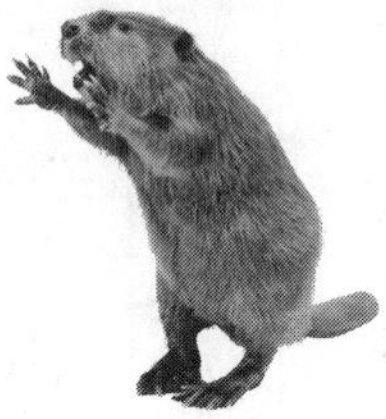
2 ______________

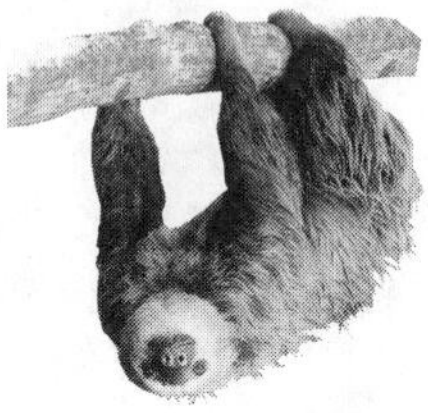
3 ______________

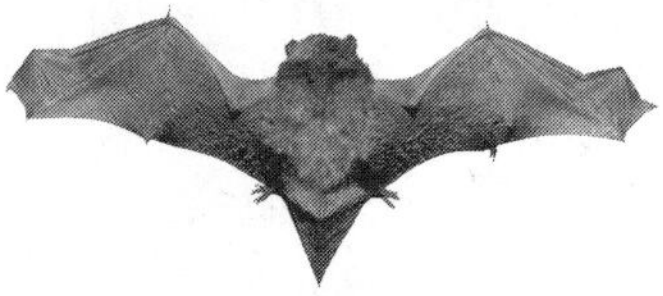
4 ______________

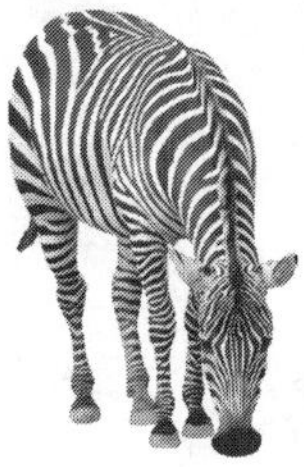
5 ______________

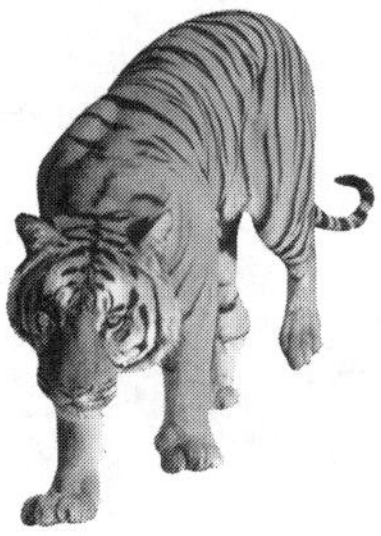
6 ______________

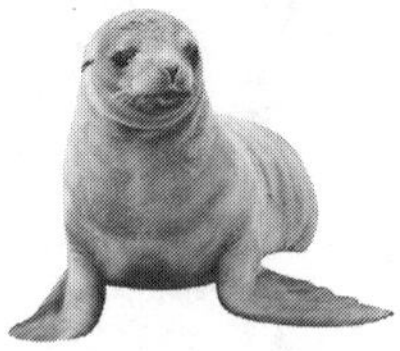
7 ______________

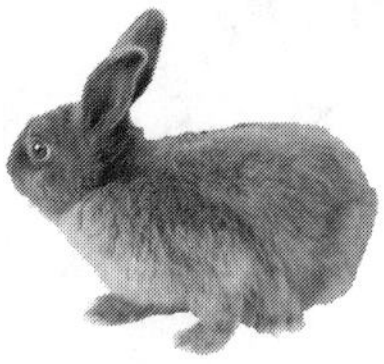
8 ______________

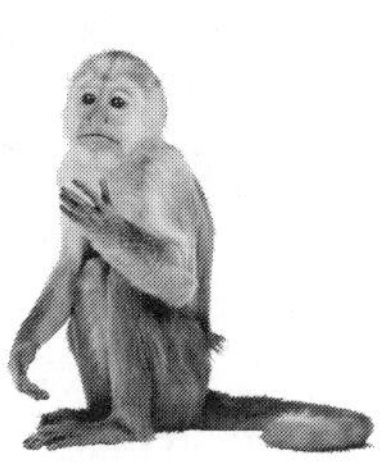
9 ______________

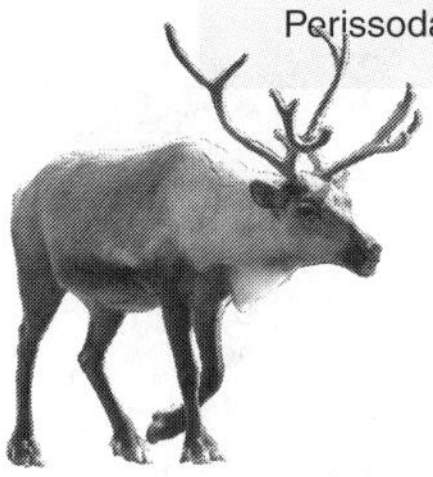
10 ______________

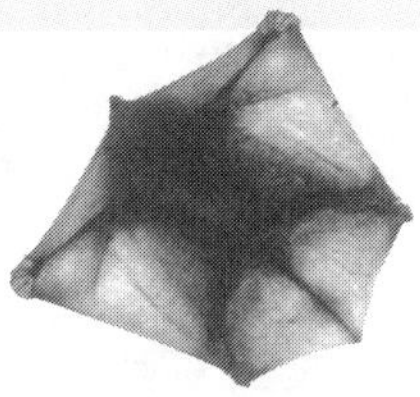
11 ______________

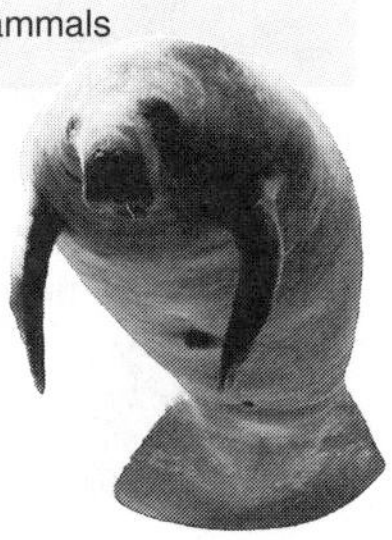
12 ______________

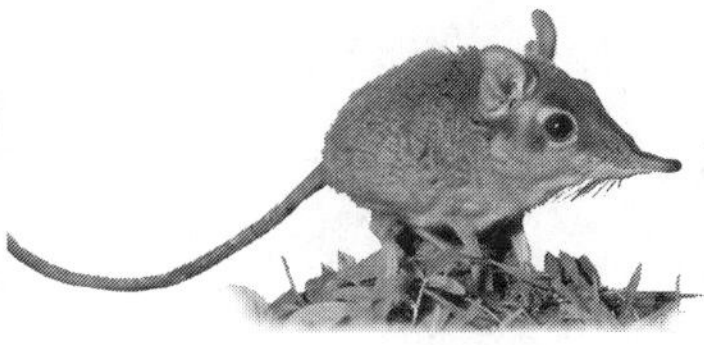
13 ______________

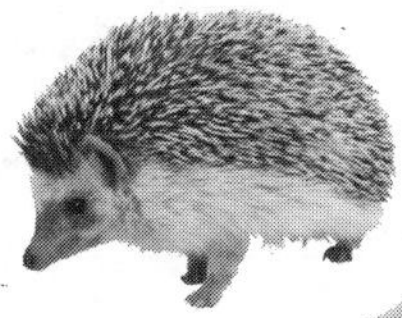
14 ______________

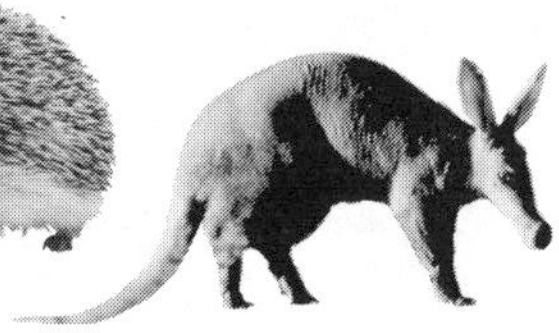
15 ______________

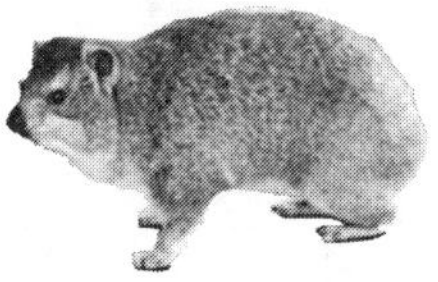
16 ______________

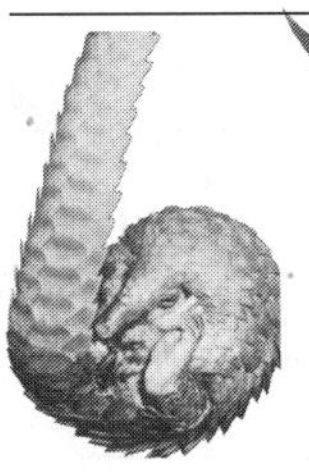
17 ______________

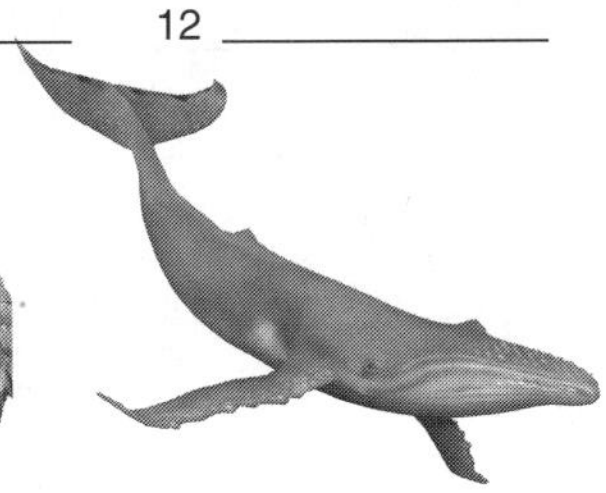
18 ______________

11. For each of three named **orders** of placental mammal, describe one **adaptive feature** that allows it to exploit a different niche from other placentals, and describe a **biological advantage** conferred by the adaptation:

(a) Order: ______________ Adaptive feature: ______________________

Biological advantage: ______________________

(b) Order: ______________ Adaptive feature: ______________________

Biological advantage: ______________________

(c) Order: ______________ Adaptive feature: ______________________

Biological advantage: ______________________

ISBN: 978-1-877462-98-6

Adaptive Radiation in Ratites

The **ratites** evolved from a single common ancestor; they are a monophyletic group of birds that lost the power of flight very early on in their evolutionary development. Ratites possess two features distinguishing them from other birds: a flat breastbone (instead of the more usual keeled shape) and a primitive palate (roof to the mouth). Flightlessness in itself is not unique to this group. There are other examples of birds that have lost the power of flight, particularly on remote, predator-free islands. Fossil evidence indicates that the ancestors of ratites were flying birds living about 80 million years ago. These ancestors also had a primitive palate, but they possessed a keeled breastbone.

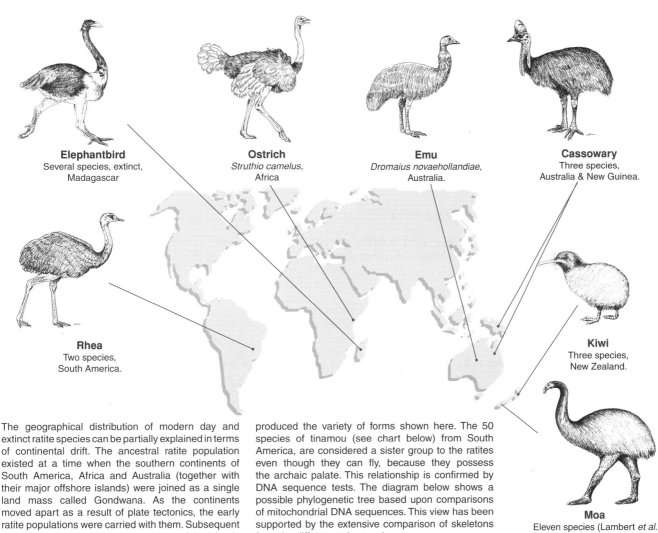

Elephantbird
Several species, extinct, Madagascar

Ostrich
Struthio camelus, Africa

Emu
Dromaius novaehollandiae, Australia.

Cassowary
Three species, Australia & New Guinea.

Rhea
Two species, South America.

Kiwi
Three species, New Zealand.

Moa
Eleven species (Lambert *et al.* 2004*), all extinct, New Zealand.

The geographical distribution of modern day and extinct ratite species can be partially explained in terms of continental drift. The ancestral ratite population existed at a time when the southern continents of South America, Africa and Australia (together with their major offshore islands) were joined as a single land mass called Gondwana. As the continents moved apart as a result of plate tectonics, the early ratite populations were carried with them. Subsequent speciation on each continent and some of the islands produced the variety of forms shown here. The 50 species of tinamou (see chart below) from South America, are considered a sister group to the ratites even though they can fly, because they possess the archaic palate. This relationship is confirmed by DNA sequence tests. The diagram below shows a possible phylogenetic tree based upon comparisons of mitochondrial DNA sequences. This view has been supported by the extensive comparison of skeletons from the different ratite species.

Mesozoic Era

Birds evolved from a saurischian (small theropod) dinosaur ancestor about 150 million years ago (below)

Ratites diverge from the line to the rest of the birds about 100 million years ago.

* Lambert *et al.* 2004. "Ancient DNA solves sex mystery of moa." Australasian Science, 25(8), Sept. 2004, pp. 14-16.

Cenozoic Era

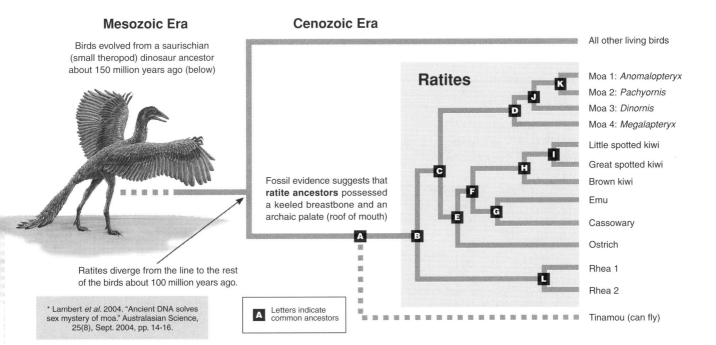

Fossil evidence suggests that **ratite ancestors** possessed a keeled breastbone and an archaic palate (roof of mouth)

A Letters indicate common ancestors

Ratites

All other living birds
Moa 1: *Anomalopteryx*
Moa 2: *Pachyornis*
Moa 3: *Dinornis*
Moa 4: *Megalapteryx*
Little spotted kiwi
Great spotted kiwi
Brown kiwi
Emu
Cassowary
Ostrich
Rhea 1
Rhea 2
Tinamou (can fly)

© BIOZONE International 2006-2012
ISBN: 978-1-877462-98-6
Photocopying Prohibited

Related activities: Patterns of Evolution, Geographical Distribution

RDA 3

1. (a) Describe three physical features distinguishing all ratities from most other birds: _____

    _____

    (b) Identify the primitive feature shared by ratites and tinamou: _____

    _____

2. Describe two anatomical changes, common to all ratites, which have evolved as a result of flightlessness. For each, describe the selection pressures for the anatomical change:

    (a) Anatomical change: _____

    Selection pressure: _____

    _____

    (b) Anatomical change: _____

    Selection pressure: _____

    _____

3. Name the ancient supercontinent that the ancestral ratite population inhabited: _____

4. (a) The extinct elephantbird from Madagascar is thought to be very closely related to another modern ratite. Based purely on the **geographical distribution** of ratites, identify the modern species that is the most likely relative:

    _____

    (b) Explain why you chose the modern ratite in your answer to (a) above: _____

    _____

    (c) Draw lines on the diagram at the bottom of the previous page to represent the divergence of the elephantbird from the modern ratite you have selected above.

5. (a) Name two other flightless birds that are not ratites: _____

    (b) Explain why these other flightless species are not considered part of the ratite group: _____

    _____

    _____

6. Eleven species of moa is an unusually large number compared to the species diversity of the kiwis, the other ratite group found in New Zealand. The moas are classified into at least four genera, whereas kiwis have only one genus. The diets of the moas and the kiwis are thought to have had a major influence on each group's capacity to diverge into separate species and genera. The moas were herbivorous, whereas kiwis are nocturnal feeders, feeding on invertebrates in the leaf litter. Explain why, on the basis of their diet, moas diverged into many species, whereas kiwis diverged little:

    _____

    _____

    _____

7. The DNA evidence suggests that New Zealand had two separate invasions of ratites, an early invasion from the moas (before the breakup of Gondwana) followed by a second invasion of the ancestors of the kiwis. Describe a possible sequence of events that could account for this:

    _____

    _____

    _____

    _____

8. The common ancestors of divergent groups are labelled (A-L) on the diagram at the bottom of the previous page. State the **letter** identifying the **common ancestor** for:

    (a) The kiwis and the Australian ratites: _____   (b) The kiwis and the moas: _____

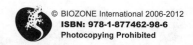 © BIOZONE International 2006-2012
ISBN: 978-1-877462-98-6
Photocopying Prohibited

Adaptive Radiation in Wrens

The New Zealand wrens have been isolated from their probable ancestral stock in Australia for more than 60 million years. Although they are called wrens because of similarities in appearance and behavior to the true wrens, they belong to an ancient suborder with no living close relatives. The endemic family to which they belong includes the rifleman, the rock wren, and the bush wren, as well as a number of extinct species. New Zealand wrens are small, insectivorous, and flightless (or with poor flying ability). The ancestral wren was almost certainly insectivorous since all the descendants are. There may well have been several related species, of which the ancestral wren was one, living in various habitats throughout early New Zealand. The existing wren family dates from a time of extensive adaptive radiation some 20 million years ago. They were once found throughout New Zealand, but their distribution is now much more restricted. Their adaptive radiation was a consequence of the break up of the New Zealand land mass during the Oligocene, (see next page), which had a profound effect on the evolution of the wrens. Earlier species, as yet undiscovered, may also have existed at this time. Although all insectivorous, the living and extinct wrens have exploited different habitats and feeding niches (see below). The fossils of extinct species can illustrate past land connections. Fossils of the Stephens Is. wren (extinct) have been found in both the North and the South Islands, showing that there was a land connection between these islands in the past. The two species of stout-legged wren may have undergone allopatric speciation 3-5 million years ago when changing sea levels separated the North and South Islands. Later similar events could also explain the evolution of separate sub-species of bush wrens and rifleman.

Curved beak wren
Spent time scurrying up and down tree trucks, probing in crevices for grubs with its curved beak.

Stout legged wren
Both species were ground dwelling, searching the ground for insects.

Stephens Is. wren
Lived and foraged in grass and underbrush (ecological equivalent of a field mouse).

Bush wren (recently extinct)
Lived and foraged in the bush searching for insects on the ground and in the air.

Rock wren
Lives in subalpine areas, feeding among rocks and tussock, and surviving winter under the snow layer.

Rifleman
Lives and feeds in the bush, picking insects from the branches and trunks of trees.

Curved beak wren

Stout legged wren

Stephens Is. wren

Bush wren

Rock wren

Rifleman

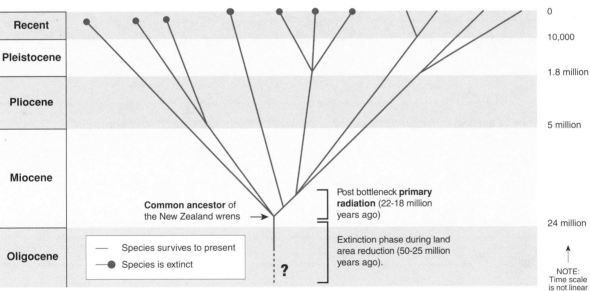

New Zealand Wren Classification

Rifleman, North Island (NI)	*Acanthisitta chloris granti*	Can fly	
Rifleman, South Island (SI)	*Acanthisitta chloris chloris*	Can fly	
Rock wren (Southern Alps)	*Xenicus gilviventris*	Can fly	
Rock wren (Fiordland)	*Xenicus gilviventris riney*	Can fly	
Bush wren (NI)	*Xenicus longipes stokesi*	Could fly	Presumed extinct
Bush wren (SI)	*Xenicus longipes longipes*	Could fly	Presumed extinct
Stead's bush wren (Stewart Is.)	*Xenicus longipes variabilis*	Could fly	Extinct
Stephens Is. wren	*Traversia lyalli*	Flightless	Extinct
Stout-legged wren (SI)	*Pachyplichas yaldwyni*	Flightless	Extinct
Stout-legged wren (NI)	*Pachyplichas jagmi*	Flightless	Extinct
Curved beak wren	*Dendroscansor decurvirostris*	Flightless	Extinct

NOTE: On the diagram, the timescale for the emergence of new sub-species, species, and genera. As a general rule among birds, new sub-species emerge after 0.5-2 million years of separation, new species after 2-10 million years, new genera after 10-20 million years and new orders with 60-80 million years of separation.

Many thanks to **Ewan Grant-Mackie**, Thames High School, and Prof. **J.A. Grant-Mackie**, Geology Dept, Auckland University, who supplied the information for this exercise.

The New Zealand Land Mass

Between 25-30 million years ago, during the Oligocene period, New Zealand was almost completely submerged, and existed only as a chain of small islands, with a land mass only 18% of what it is today. This was the result of rising sea levels and land subsidence over a period of 5 million years.

The New Zealand Wrens

The reduction in size and break-up of the single land mass had a profound effect on the evolution of the wrens, greatly reducing their range of habitats and causing selective extinctions:

- *The reduction in species diversity*
  When the New Zealand land mass was inundated during the Oligocene, some animals would have retreated to islands of high ground, but would have perished as these became submerged. As a result, a great many species were lost (species diversity declined).

- *The reduction in genetic diversity*
  Not only was species diversity lost during this period, the genetic diversity of remaining populations would have been severely depleted, with few individuals in a species surviving to pass on their genes. This situation, referred to as a **population bottleneck**, occurs when a very small sample of the total species gene pool manages to survive.

When the sea levels dropped again, the survivors moved into new areas to occupy newly available niches.

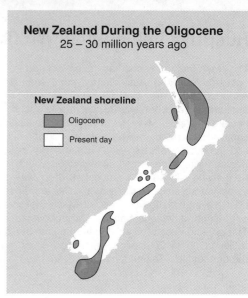

New Zealand During the Oligocene
25 – 30 million years ago

New Zealand shoreline
- Oligocene
- Present day

1. Adaptive radiations have occurred on several occasions in the New Zealand wrens:

    (a) What is the difference between **primary radiation** and **secondary radiation**? _____

    _____

    _____

    (b) When did the primary radiation occur following the population bottleneck? _____

    (c) When did the secondary radiation occur? _____

    (d) On the diagram on the previous page, mark with brackets the secondary radiation of wrens.

2. The wrens have undergone two periods where extinctions have occurred; an early one more than 25 million years ago, followed by a recent extinction phase.

    (a) What event caused the **early extinction** phase? _____

    _____

    (b) What was the most likely cause for the **recent extinction** phase of some of the wren species? _____

    _____

    _____

3. Describe the niche of each wren, including reference to the way in which they may have differentiated:

    (a) Rock wren: _____

    _____

    (b) Bush wren: _____

    _____

    (c) Stephens Island wren: _____

    _____

    (d) Curved beak wren: _____

    _____

    (e) Rifleman: _____

    _____

4. Explain how geological events in New Zealand affected the radiation of the wrens: _____

    _____

    _____

Origin of New Zealand Parrots

Mitochondrial **DNA** (mtDNA) studies at Victoria University (Wellington, New Zealand) confirm the existence in New Zealand of two distinct groups of parrots: kakapo-kaka-kea, and the various kakariki (five species). This research provides an excellent example of the use of **DNA analysis** to determine evolutionary relationships. The first group originated from an, as yet unknown, Australian ancestor about 100 million years ago (mya). This proto-kaka/kakapo formed as a consequence of the break-up of Gondwana, when New Zealand moved away in isolation from the Australian landmass. The kakapo split from this lineage 60-80 mya and is today our most ancient parrot.

Kaka split from the kea line some 3 mya and an early member migrated to produce the now-extinct Norfolk Island kaka. About 400,000 years ago the North and South Island kaka diverged. Mitochondrial DNA studies also show that the second group of New Zealand's parrots, the kakariki, are most likely derived from a New Caledonian parakeet ancestor, which in turn was derived at some time from an unknown Australian ancestor (possibly a proto-rosella). After the ancestral kakariki arrived in New Zealand, probably via Norfolk or Lord Howe Islands, it speciated by migration and geographic isolation (a process known as **vicariance**), and by ecological and behavioral divergence.

Kaka (*Nestor meridionalis*) has a North Island and a South Island subspecies. They feed on fruit, honeydew, and insects.

Kea (*Nestor notabilis*) inhabits mountain regions of the South Island. They feed on fruit and insects, and are also scavengers.

Kakapo (*Strigops habroptilus*) is a ground-dwelling (flightless) night parrot that was once widely distributed throughout Fiordland and Stewart Island. They feed on berry fruit.

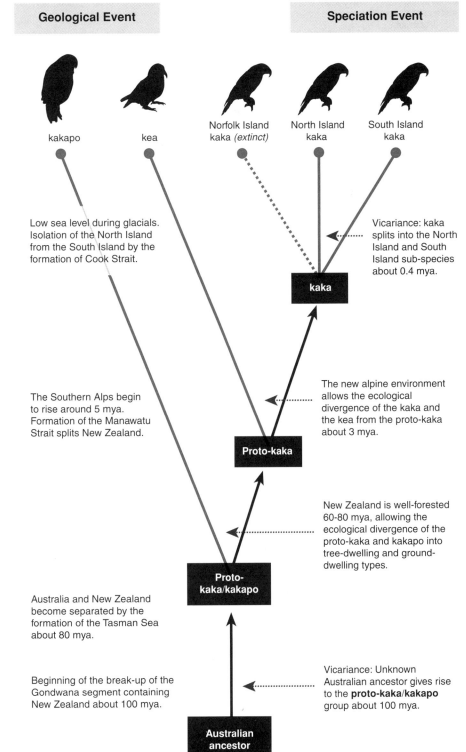

Geological Event

Speciation Event

kakapo   kea   Norfolk Island kaka (*extinct*)   North Island kaka   South Island kaka

Low sea level during glacials. Isolation of the North Island from the South Island by the formation of Cook Strait.

Vicariance: kaka splits into the North Island and South Island sub-species about 0.4 mya.

kaka

The Southern Alps begin to rise around 5 mya. Formation of the Manawatu Strait splits New Zealand.

The new alpine environment allows the ecological divergence of the kaka and the kea from the proto-kaka about 3 mya.

Proto-kaka

New Zealand is well-forested 60-80 mya, allowing the ecological divergence of the proto-kaka and kakapo into tree-dwelling and ground-dwelling types.

Proto-kaka/kakapo

Australia and New Zealand become separated by the formation of the Tasman Sea about 80 mya.

Beginning of the break-up of the Gondwana segment containing New Zealand about 100 mya.

Vicariance: Unknown Australian ancestor gives rise to the **proto-kaka/kakapo** group about 100 mya.

Australian ancestor (unknown)

Source: E.J. Grant-Mackie (Thames High School) and J.A. Grant-Mackie (Geology Dept, University of Auckland), based on mDNA studies by Prof. Geoff Chambers and Dr Wee Ming Boon (Victoria University of Wellington).

 *Periodicals:* Evolution in New Zealand

Related activities: Ancient Landscapes
Weblinks: New Zealand Evolutionary Evidence

RA 2

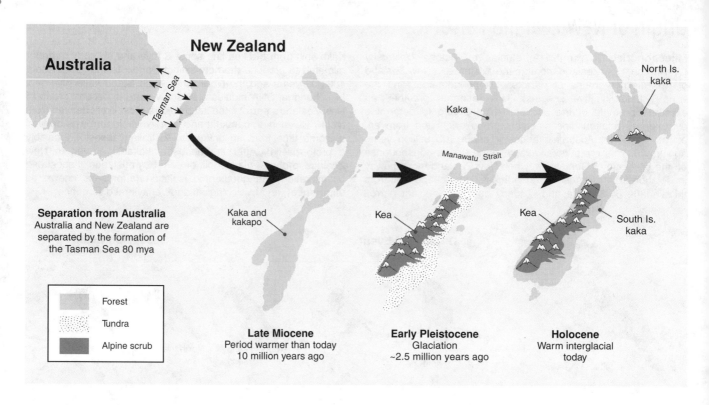

Separation from Australia
Australia and New Zealand are
separated by the formation of
the Tasman Sea 80 mya

Forest

Tundra

Alpine scrub

Late Miocene
Period warmer than today
10 million years ago

Early Pleistocene
Glaciation
~2.5 million years ago

Holocene
Warm interglacial
today

1. What role did **geographical isolation** play in the divergence of the proto-kaka/kakapo from its Australian ancestor?

_____

_____

_____

2. (a) Describe the two habitats in which the kaka and kea species evolved: _____

_____

_____

(b) When did these two different habitats emerge? _____

(c) How could the kaka and the kea have evolved from an ancestral proto-kaka? _____

_____

_____

3. Identify the species that became cold-adapted: _____

4. Why do the modern kaka and kea species in the South Island not interbreed? _____

_____

_____

_____

5. It has previously been postulated that the kakapo may be related to the Australian night parrots and/or Australian ground
   parrots, but this has not been supported by modern DNA studies. Suggest a reason for the similarities (appearance,
   ground nesting, poor flight) between these Australian parrots and the kakapo:

_____

_____

_____

6. The kakapo is described as our most ancient parrot. Why do they deserve this label? _____

_____

Evolution in Springtails

Genetic analysis is now widely used to investigate dispersal and divergence in all kinds of species. Springtails are tiny arthropods and have a limited capacity to move between locations. For this reason, they are good candidates for studying evolutionary phenomena. Researchers wanted to investigate the genetic relatedness of springtails in a Dry Valley in Antarctica. Results of a mtDNA study show two distinct genetic 'types' of springtail in Taylor Valley (see map, black and white squares on the following page). The two types have different DNA bases at a number of positions in a mitochondrial gene. They also coexist in an area

of **sympatry** in the middle of Taylor Valley. The results of the research are summarized below. It shows an order of separation based on the genetic differences between the two types (TV1-14) compared with other populations of the same species (from Cape Evans, Cape Royds, and Beaufort Is). One other Antarctic species of springtail (*Biscoia sudpolaris*) is included on the diagram as an 'outgroup' (reference point). The genetic difference between populations is indicated by the distance to the 'branching point'. Groups that branch apart early in the tree are more different genetically than groups that branch later.

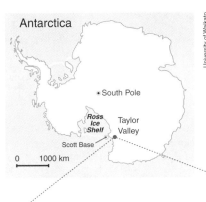

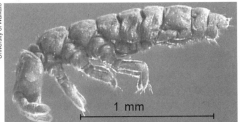

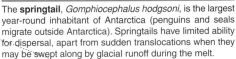

The **springtail**, *Gomphiocephalus hodgsoni*, is the largest year-round inhabitant of Antarctica (penguins and seals migrate outside Antarctica). Springtails have limited ability for dispersal, apart from sudden translocations when they may be swept along by glacial runoff during the melt.

Genetic relationship between samples of springtail *Gomphiocephalus hodgsoni* in Taylor Valley, Antarctica

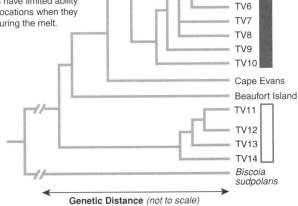

Taylor Valley (above) is one of the Dry Valleys in Antarctica, and is clear of snow virtually the whole year round. Any snow that falls in it soon melts as the dark rock surface heats up in the sun.

Source: Many thanks to Liam Nolan, teacher at Tauranga Girls' College, for supplying the information for these pages. Liam studied with the **Center for Biodiversity and Ecology Research** (University of Waikato), whilst the recipient of a study award from the Ministry of Education.

This photo taken in **Taylor Valley** (above) shows an ephemeral stream (it dries up at certain times of the year) emerging from one of the many "hanging glaciers" that line the margins of the valley. Such streams provide the moisture essential for springtails to survive amongst rocks, moss, lichen, and algae.

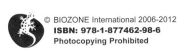

Mosses (left) are the tallest plants in Antarctica. They provide ideal habitats for springtails. Although springtails have antifreeze (glycerol) in their blood, they are still vulnerable to freezing. Antarctic springtails do not possess the proteins that some Antarctic fish have to help them avoid freezing.

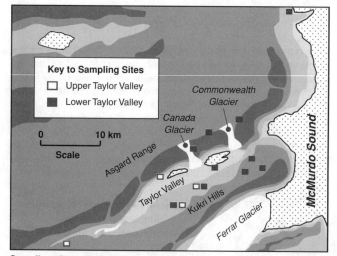

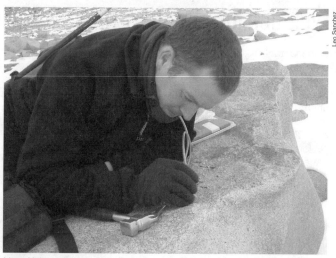

Sampling sites: A total of 14 sampling sites was used to build up a picture of the genetic diversity of springtails in an area of Taylor Valley. They were named TV1 through TV14 (TV = Taylor Valley). Black squares represent one genetic 'type' of springtail, while white squares represent another.

Liam Nolan uses a pooter to suck up springtails disturbed from their hiding places between the flakes of rock covering a boulder. The samples collected in Taylor Valley, were brought back to the "lab tent" at the camp, where they were preserved and prepared for their return to New Zealand.

1. Study the diagram of genetic relationships between samples of springtails (on the previous page). Describe what you notice about the branching point of the populations from the upper (TV11-14) and lower (TV1-10) Taylor Valley:

   _____

   _____

2. Studies of the enzymes from the two 'types' of springtails indicate that the springtails do not interbreed. Explain why this is significant:

   _____

   _____

3. Springtails cannot fly and in Antarctica quickly dry out and die if they are blown by the wind. Discuss the significance of these two features for gene flow between populations:

   _____

   _____

4. Isolated populations of springtails are often small. Describe the mechanism that could be important in increasing genetic difference between such populations:

   _____

   _____

   _____

5. Taylor Valley was once (thousands of years ago) covered in ice, with the only habitats available for springtails being the mountain tops lining both sides of the valley. Explain how this, together with low dispersal rates and small population size, could result in the formation of two species from one original species of springtail:

   _____

   _____

   _____

   _____

6. Discuss what could be done in Taylor Valley in order to conserve the biodiversity of springtails:

   _____

   _____

   _____

   _____

Ancient Landscapes

Adaptive radiations are a feature of the biota of archipelagos, such as the Hawaiian islands. Periodic cycles of volcanic activity, fragmentation, and sea level change can isolate founder populations and expose them to new selection pressures, accelerating the pace of evolutionary change. The evolution of New Zealand's flora and fauna provides a good example of this. New Zealand's fragmentation into islands (~30 mya), cooling climate (from ~10 mya), and increasingly mountainous landscape (from ~5 mya) has been associated with many speciation events and has led to a rich diversity of endemic species.

Warm Interglacial Periods

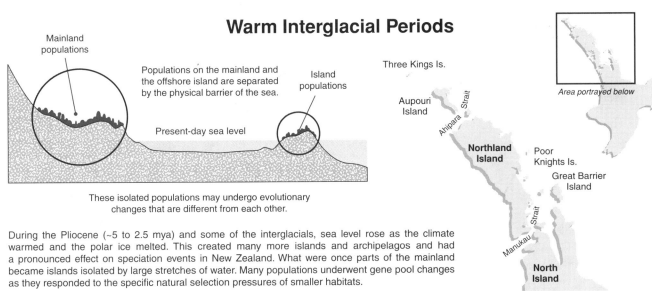

These isolated populations may undergo evolutionary changes that are different from each other.

During the Pliocene (~5 to 2.5 mya) and some of the interglacials, sea level rose as the climate warmed and the polar ice melted. This created many more islands and archipelagos and had a pronounced effect on speciation events in New Zealand. What were once parts of the mainland became islands isolated by large stretches of water. Many populations underwent gene pool changes as they responded to the specific natural selection pressures of smaller habitats.

Glacial Periods

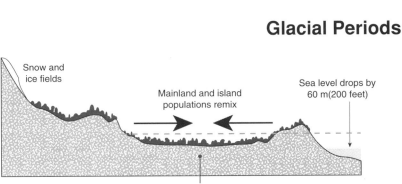

The sea bed is exposed for thousands of years and is recolonized by terrestrial organisms.

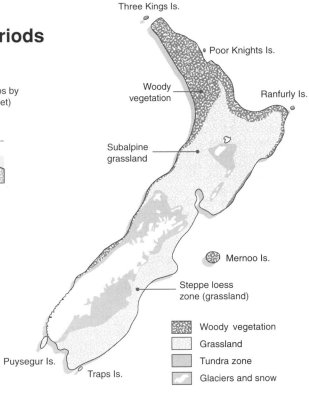

During the last glacial, 20,000-18,000 years ago, New Zealand's shoreline was approximately 60 m lower than it is today. The exposed seabed would have been colonized by organisms over a period of time. The majority of the landmass was covered by snowfields or grasslands. The podocarp forests, which covered most of the North Island in more recent times, were restricted to north of Auckland and along the coastline in some regions (the sea has a moderating effect on local climate). The southern cool-temperate beech forests were widespread. Large areas of the exposed seabed are thought to have been covered by this forest.

Significance: During this phase, the distribution ranges of many species were altered. New climatic conditions altered habitat, in some cases drastically, and generated new selection pressures. There was opportunity for species to increase their distribution to what would later become offshore islands.

The diagram above shows New Zealand during a glacial period with the sea level 60 m below present level, revealing large areas of sea bed.

1. Explain how the interglacial periods contributed to speciation events in New Zealand: _____

_____

_____

2. Explain how the glacial periods contributed to speciation events in New Zealand: _____

_____

_____

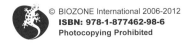

© BIOZONE International 2006-2012
ISBN: 978-1-877462-98-6
Photocopying Prohibited

Periodicals: Evolution in New Zealand

Related activities: Evolution in New Zealand Invertebrates
Weblinks: New Zealand Evolutionary Evidence

A 2

Evolution in New Zealand Invertebrates

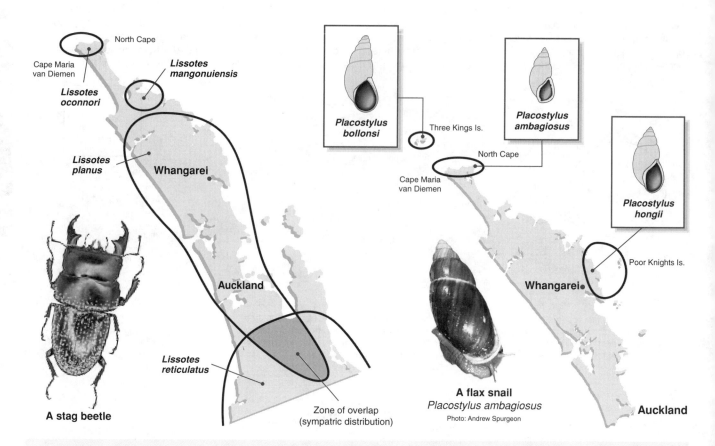

A stag beetle

A flax snail
Placostylus ambagiosus
Photo: Andrew Spurgeon

Zone of overlap
(sympatric distribution)

Stag Beetles

The four species of closely related stag beetles found in the upper North Island are thought to have shared a common ancestor prior to the Pliocene rise in sea level. When the climate warmed and the sea level rose, a chain of islands (an archipelago) was created, isolating parts of the population. Over thousands of years of isolation with different selection pressures, each group developed separate species status. Since the fall in sea level, these populations have been able to remix in many cases, but the gene pool of the species remains intact because reproductive isolating mechanisms have developed. The point of origin for each species can be estimated by comparing their present distribution with that of Pliocene Northland.

Flax Snails

The large, herbivorous land snails of the genus *Placostylus* are found on islands elsewhere in the southern Pacific Ocean, but in New Zealand they are restricted to localities in the North Auckland Peninsula and off-lying island conservation reserves. The present conservation status of these three species is considered to be endangered. This is largely due to their sudden exposure to new selection pressures in the form of reduced or modified habitat and the introduction of mammalian predators (e.g. the Polynesian rat and the European ship and black rats). They have no natural defenses against these very efficient hunters and intensive predator controls are necessary if their populations are to recover.

1. Consult the map of the Northland region during the Pliocene (see the activity *Ancient New Zealand Landscapes*) and try to determine the possible origin of each of the **stag beetle** and **flax snail** species in terms of their geographic isolation (i.e. what land mass were they restricted to during their development as a separate species).

   (a) *L. oconnori*: _____

   (b) *L. mangonuiensis*: _____

   (c) *L. planus*: _____

   (d) *L. reticulatus*: _____

   (e) *P. bollonsi*: _____

   (f) *P. ambagiosus*: _____

   (g) *P. hongii*: _____

2. (a) Identify the two species of stag beetle that are sympatric in their distribution: _____

   _____

   (b) Describe the likely event that allowed these two species to occupy the same region south of Auckland:

   _____

© BIOZONE International 2006-2012
ISBN: 978-1-877462-98-6
Photocopying Prohibited

RA 3

Related activities: *Allopatric Speciation*
Weblinks: *New Zealand Evolutionary Evidence*

Human Intervention in Evolution

Key concepts

▶ Humans can alter the genotype and phenotype of organisms by selective breeding.

▶ Human use of chemicals such as antibiotics and insecticides create a selective environment that has influenced the evolution of some taxa such as bacteria and insects.

▶ Human alteration of the environment through pollution, climate change, and habitat loss may change the selection pressures on natural populations of organisms.

Objectives

☐ 1. Use the **KEY TERMS** to help you understand and complete these objectives.

Selective Breeding pages 108-114

☐ 2. Explain what is meant by **artificial selection** (also called **selective breeding**). Compare and contrast artificial selection and natural selection.

☐ 3. Describe how artificial selection has created phenotypic and genotypic change in populations. Examples include:
   • The development of modern livestock breeds from their wild ancestors. Recent technologies such as artificial insemination and marker assisted selection are accelerating the rate of change in some species.
   • The development of crop varieties, including bread wheat, from their wild ancestors. Explain the role of special genetic events, such as **polyploidy**, in the development of many modern crop varieties.

The Evolution of Resistance pages 115-119

☐ 4. Identify examples of drug and pesticide resistance in organisms. Explain the role of human activity in enhancing the selective environment for the development or spread of resistance to specific chemicals.

☐ 5. Describe the origin of antibiotic resistance in bacteria. Explain how bacteria transfer drug resistance between generations by **vertical gene transmission**. Distinguish this from **horizontal gene transmission**, involving gene transfer by **conjugation**. Recognize that the genes for antibiotic resistance are not new, but are becoming relatively more common in the current selective environment. Explain how humans can alter this selective environment.

☐ 6. Describe the origin of chloroquine resistance in the malaria parasite. Explain how the selective environment for chloroquine resistance arose, how it was maintained, and how it has recently changed.

☐ 7. Describe the origin and occurrence of drug resistance in viruses, e.g. HIV and influenza. Explain how human behavior contributes to a selective environment that favors the spread of drug resistance.

☐ 8. Describe the origin, occurrence, and spread of insecticide resistance in a named insect. Explain why some insecticides are returning as effective control agents in some cases. What does this tell us about the evolution of populations and the role of environment in evolutionary change?

Humans and the Changing Environment pages 120-121

☐ 9. Use an example, e.g. **pollution**, habitat loss, or **climate change**, to discuss the role of human induced environmental change in the evolution of natural populations. Explain how changing environments alter selection pressures in different ways for different species and describe the consequences of this for **biodiversity**, **genetic diversity**, and ecosystem health.

Periodicals:
Listings for this chapter are on page 123

Weblinks:
www.thebiozone.com/
weblink/Evol-2986.html

Presentation Media
EVOLUTION:
Evolution

Darwin: Pigeon Fancier?

The rock pigeon: a versatile progenitor

The rock pigeon or rock dove (Columba livia) includes the domestic pigeon (including the fancy pigeons on which Darwin worked) and domestic pigeons which become feral. It is a highly adaptable species and shows a range of phenotypes. Feral pigeons for example show many different plumage colorations.

Pigeon Fanciers and Selective Breeding

"*... from so simple a beginning endless forms most beautiful and most wonderful have been, and are being evolved.*" This quotation closes Charles Darwin's most famous work "*The Origin of Species by Means of Natural Selection*". Most students of biology know of Darwin's voyage aboard *The Beagle*" and his precise and careful documenting of the variety of species he encountered on his travels, to the Galápagos in particular. But the naturalist's careful attention to biological detail extended to his work at home in England. Darwin began to formulate his theory of evolution during his five year voyage aboard *The Beagle*, but this work continued in earnest when he returned home to England and established a home (and research station) at Down House. Darwin delayed publishing his greatest work, fearing ridicule in the deeply religious English society. He wanted to gather more evidence to support his idea that species could change. He found this evidence by studying domesticated species that he knew could be shaped through breeding. Pigeons, rabbits, cabbages, gooseberries; these organisms would become his window into the workings of selection. Thus Darwin became a pigeon fancier. Indeed, the humble pigeon, loved by generations of English people, played a most important part in his work on both 'The Origin of Species' (1859) and 'Variation in Domestication' (1868). He said "*Believing that it is always best to study some special group, I have ... taken up domestic pigeons.*"

Darwin excelled in careful observation and meticulous record keeping and he was a frequent correspondent with like-minded thinkers. As well as breeding his own pigeons, he managed to secure skins and skeletons from colleagues and acquaintances all over Britain. But Darwin was interested in evolution, not pigeon shows. He wanted a sense of how much variation existed within a single species in nature and saw selective breeding as a "speeded up version" of the process that gave rise to new species in nature. Darwin's pigeon work was much more than a hobby; it was a way to get his point across and to demonstrate the dramatic effects of selection. Darwin skeletonized and meticulously recorded the details of hundreds of specimens and concluded that if artificial selection could produce such diversity over decades, what might natural selection produce over millions of years?

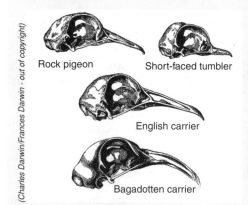

Skulls of various pigeon breeds as drawn by Darwin. Relative sizes accurate. Darwin noted that difference in breed appearance extended even to the skeletal features.

Pouters: This group includes breeds developed for the ability to inflate their crops. The pygmy pouter's bizarre appearance has made it one of the least popular breeds, except in shows.

The fantail is characterized by a fan-shaped tail composed of 30 to 40 feathers; more than most members of the pigeon family, which usually have only 12 to 14 feathers. A feather mutation called silky produces yet another variety.

1. Explain why Darwin sought support for his evolutionary theory from his pigeon breeding work: _____

_____

2. Explain why his findings supported his ideas that species could change over time: _____

Selective Breeding in Animals

The domestication of livestock has a long history dating back at least 8000 years. Today's important stock breeds were all derived from wild ancestors that were domesticated by humans, who then used **selective breeding** to produce livestock to meet specific requirements. Selective breeding of domesticated animals involves identifying desirable qualities (e.g. high wool production or meat yield), and breeding together individuals with those qualities so the trait is reliably passed on. Practices such as **inbreeding**, **line-breeding**, and **outcrossing** are used to select and 'fix' desirable traits in varieties. Today, modern breeding techniques often employ reproductive technologies, such as

artificial insemination, so that the desirable characteristics of one male can be passed on to many females. These new technologies refine the selection process and increase the rate at which stock improvements are made. Rates are predicted to accelerate further as new technologies, such as genomic selection, become more widely available and less costly. However, producing highly inbred lines of animals with specific traits can have disadvantages. **Homozygosity** for a number of desirable traits can cause physiological or physical problems to the animal itself. For example, animals bred specifically for rapid weight gain often grow so fast that they have skeletal and muscular difficulties.

The Origin of Domestic Animals

PIG
Wild ancestor: Boar
Origin: Anatolia, 9000 years BP
Now: More than 12 distinct modern breeds, including the Berkshire (meat) and Tamworth (hardiness).

DOMESTIC FOWL
Wild ancestor: Red jungle fowl
Origin: Indus Valley, 4000 BP
Now: More than 60 breeds including Rhode Island Red (meat) and Leghorn (egg production).

Each domesticated breed has been bred from the wild ancestor (pictured). The date indicates the earliest record of the domesticated form (years before present or BP). Different countries have different criteria for selection, based on their local environments and consumer preferences.

GOAT
Wild ancestor: Bezoar goat
Origin: Iraq, 10,000 years BP
Now: approx. 35 breeds including Spanish (meat), Angora (fibre) and Nubian (dairy).

SHEEP
Wild ancestor: Asiatic mouflon
Origin: Iran, Iraq, Levant, 10,000 years BP
Now: More than 200 breeds including Merino (wool), Suffolk (meat), Friesian (milk), and dual purpose (Romney).

CATTLE
Wild ancestor: Auroch (extinct)
Origin: SW Asia, 10,000 years BP
Now: 800 modern breeds including the Aberdeen angus (meat), Friesian and Jersey (milk), and Zebu (draught).

Human Intervention in Evolution

1. Distinguish between inbreeding and out-crossing, explaining the significance of each technique in selective breeding:

2. How are new reproductive technologies contributing to rapid phenotypic change in populations?

© BIOZONE International 2006-2011
ISBN: 978-1-877462-98-6
Photocopying Prohibited

Periodicals: Taming the wild

Related activities: Selective Breeding in Crop Plants
Weblinks: Dogs and More Dogs

RA 2

Dogs provide a striking example of selective breeding, with more than 400 recognized breeds. Over centuries, humans have selected for desirable physical and behavioral traits. All breeds of dog are members of the same species, **Canis familiaris**. This species descended from a single wild species, the gray wolf **Canis lupus**, over 15,000 years ago. Five ancient dog breeds are recognized, from which all other breeds are thought to have descended by artificial selection.

Gray wolf *Canis lupus pallipes*

The gray wolf is distributed throughout Europe, North America, and Asia. Amongst members of this species, there is a lot of variation in coat coloration. This accounts for the large variation in coat colours of dogs today.

The Ancestor of Domestic Dogs

Until recently, it was unclear whether the ancestor to the modern domestic dogs was the desert wolf of the Middle East, the woolly wolf of central Asia, or the gray wolf of Northern Hemisphere. Recent genetic studies (mitochondrial DNA comparisons) now provide strong evidence that the ancestor of domestic dogs throughout the world is the gray wolf. It seems likely that this evolutionary change took place in a single region, most probably China.

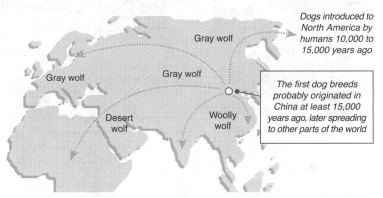

Dogs introduced to North America by humans 10,000 to 15,000 years ago

Gray wolf

Gray wolf

Gray wolf

Desert wolf

Woolly wolf

The first dog breeds probably originated in China at least 15,000 years ago, later spreading to other parts of the world

Mastiff-type
Canis familiaris inostranzevi

Originally from Tibet, the first records of this breed of dog go back to the Stoneage.

Grayhound
Canis familiaris leineri

Drawings of this breed on pottery dated from 8000 years ago in the Middle East make it one of the oldest.

Pointer-type
Canis familiaris intermedius

Probably derived from the grayhound breed for the purpose of hunting small game.

Sheepdog
Canis familiaris metris optimae

Originating in Europe, this breed has been used to guard flocks from predators for thousands of years.

Wolf-like
Canis familiaris palustris

Found in snow covered habitats in northern Europe, Asia (Siberia), and North America (Alaska).

3. How has selective breeding contributed to changes in the gene pool of domestic dogs? _____

_____

_____

_____

4. Which behavioral characteristics of wolves predisposed them to successful domestication? _____

_____

_____

_____

5. List the physical and behavioral traits that would be desirable (selected for) in the following uses of a dog:

    (a) Hunting large game (e.g. boar and deer): _____

    (b) Game fowl dog: _____

    (c) Stock control (sheep/cattle dog): _____

    (d) Family pet (house dog): _____

    (e) Guard dog: _____

Selective Breeding in Crop Plants

For thousands of years, farmers have used the variation in wild and cultivated plants to develop crops. Genetic diversity gives species the ability to adapt to new environmental challenges, such as new pests, diseases, or growing conditions. The genetic diversity within different crop varieties provides options to develop, through selection, new and more productive crop plants.

Brassica oleracea is a good example of the variety that can be produced by selectively growing plants with desirable traits. Not only are there six varieties of *Brassica oleracea*, but each of those has a number of sub varieties as well. Although brassicas have been cultivated for several thousand years, cauliflower, broccoli and brussels sprouts appeared only in the last 500 years.

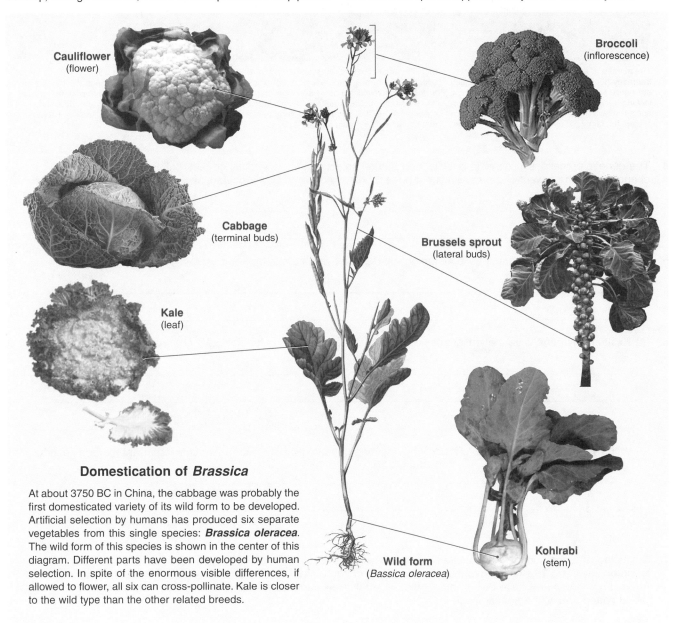

Cauliflower (flower)

Broccoli (inflorescence)

Cabbage (terminal buds)

Brussels sprout (lateral buds)

Kale (leaf)

Kohlrabi (stem)

Wild form (*Bassica oleracea*)

Domestication of *Brassica*

At about 3750 BC in China, the cabbage was probably the first domesticated variety of its wild form to be developed. Artificial selection by humans has produced six separate vegetables from this single species: **Brassica oleracea**. The wild form of this species is shown in the center of this diagram. Different parts have been developed by human selection. In spite of the enormous visible differences, if allowed to flower, all six can cross-pollinate. Kale is closer to the wild type than the other related breeds.

1. Study the diagram above and identify which part of the plant has been selected for to produce each of the vegetables:

   (a) Cauliflower: _____

   (b) Kale: _____

   (c) Broccoli: _____

   (d) Brussels sprout: _____

   (e) Cabbage: _____

   (f) Kohlrabi: _____

2. Describe the feature of these vegetables that suggests they are members of the same species: _____

   _____

3. Describe the method used to develop broccoli and the features one would look for when doing so: _____

   _____

   _____

The number of apple varieties is now a fraction of the many hundreds grown a century ago. Apples are native to Kazakhstan and breeders are now looking back to this center of diversity to develop apples resistant to the bacterial disease that causes fire blight.

In 18th-century Ireland, potatoes were the main source of food for about 30% of the population, and farmers relied almost entirely on one very fertile and productive variety. That variety proved susceptible to the potato blight fungus which resulted in a widespread famine.

Hybrid corn varieties have been bred to minimize harm inflicted by insect pests such as corn rootworm (above). Hybrids are important because they recombine the genetic characteristics of parental lines and show increased heterozygosity and hybrid vigor.

4. The genetic processes involved in artificial and natural selection are essentially no different. Explain how this has changed with the advent of genetic engineering technology and why it is particularly relevant to crop plants:

_____

_____

5. Describe a phenotypic characteristic that might be desirable in an apple tree and explain your choice:

_____

_____

6. (a) Explain why genetic diversity might decline during selective breeding for particular characteristics:

_____

_____

_____

(b) With reference to an example, discuss why retaining genetic diversity in crop plants is important for food security:

_____

_____

_____

7. Cultivated American cotton plants have a total of 52 chromosomes (2N = 52). In each cell there are 26 large chromosomes and 26 small chromosomes. Old World cotton plants have 26 chromosomes (2N = 26), all large. Wild American cotton plants have 26 chromosomes, all small. How might cultivated American cotton have originated from Old World cotton and wild American cotton:

_____

_____

8. The Cavendish is the variety of banana most commonly sold in world supermarkets. It is seedless, sterile, and under threat of extinction by Panama disease Race 4. Explain why Cavendish banana crops are so endangered by this fungus:

_____

_____

_____

9. Discuss the need to maintain the biodiversity of wild plants and ancient farm breeds: _____

_____

_____

_____

© BIOZONE International 2006-2012
ISBN: 978-1-877462-98-6
Photocopying Prohibited

Breeding Modern Wheat

Wheat has been cultivated for more than 9000 years and has undergone many genetic changes during its domestication. The evolution of modern bread wheat from its wild ancestors (below) involved two natural **hybridization** events, accompanied by polyploidy. Once wheat became domesticated, artificial selection under cultivation emphasized characteristics such as high protein (gluten) content, high yield, and pest resistance to pests and disease. Hybrid vigor in wheat cultivars is produced by crossing inbred lines and selecting for desirable traits in the progeny, which can now be identified using genetic techniques such as marker assisted selection. This is an indirect selection process where a trait of interest is selected on the basis of a marker linked to it. Increasingly, research is focused on enhancing the genetic diversity of wheat to provide for future crop development. With this in mind, there is renewed interest in some of the lower yielding, ancient wheat varieties, such as wild emmer, Kamut®, and spelt, which pre-date common wheat. Not only do these older varieties offer a broader spectrum of nutrients than common and durum wheat, but they contain alleles no longer present in modern inbred varieties.

The Evolution and Domestication of Wheat

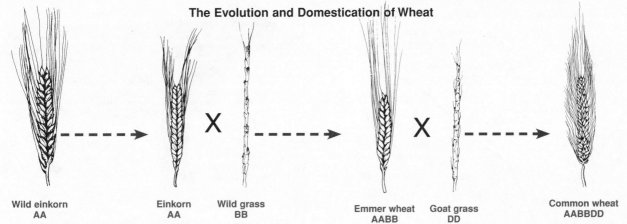

Wild einkorn AA → **Einkorn AA** X **Wild grass BB** → **Emmer wheat AABB** **Goat grass DD** → **Common wheat AABBDD**

Wild einkorn becomes domesticated in the Middle East. There are slight changes to phenotype but not chromosome number.

A sterile hybrid between einkorn and wild grass undergoes a chromosome doubling to create fertile emmer wheat.

A sterile hybrid between emmer wheat and goat grass undergoes a chromosome doubling to create fertile common wheat.

Ancient cereal grasses had heads which shattered easily so that the seeds were widely scattered. In this more primitive morphology, the wheat ear breaks into spikelets when threshed, and milling or pounding is needed to remove the hulls and obtain the grain. Cultivation and repeated harvesting and sowing of the grains of wild grasses led to domestic strains with larger seeds and sturdier heads. Modern selection methods incorporate genetic techniques to identify and isolate beneficial genes, e.g. the RHt dwarfing gene, which gave rise to shorter stemmed modern wheat varieties.

Modern bread wheat has been selected for its non-shattering heads, high yield, and high gluten (protein) content. The grains are larger and the seeds (spikelets) remain attached to the ear by a toughened rachis during harvesting. On threshing, the chaff breaks up, releasing the grains. Selection for these traits by farmers might not necessarily have been deliberate, but occurred because these traits made it easier to gather the seeds. Such **'incidental' selection** was an important part of crop domestication. **Hybrid vigor** in cultivars is generated by crossing inbred lines.

Durum wheat is a modern variety developed by artificial selection of the domesticated emmer wheat strains. Durum (also called hard wheat) has large firm kernels with a high protein content. These properties make it suitable for pasta production. As with all new wheat varieties, new cultivars are produced by crossing two lines using hand pollination, then selfing or **inbreeding** the progeny that combine the desirable traits of both parents. Progeny are evaluated for several years for the traits of interest, until they can be released as established varieties or cultivars.

1. Describe three phenotypic characteristics that would be desirable in a wheat plant:

   (a) _____

   (b) _____

   (c) _____

2. Explain how both natural events and artificial selection have contributed to the high yielding modern wheat varieties:

   _____

   _____

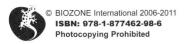
Related activities: Selective Breeding in Crop Plants

RA 2

Designer Herds

Most of the economically important traits in dairy cattle are quantitative traits, i.e. they are traits that are affected by many genes, as well as environment. The most important traits (below right) are expressed only in females, but the main opportunity for selection is in males. Intense selection of the best bulls, combined with their worldwide use through **artificial insemination** and frozen semen has seen a rapid genetic gain in dairy cattle since the 1970s. Bulls are assigned statistically-determined and unbiased **breeding values** based on the performance of their daughters and granddaughters. In this way, the bulls and cows with the best genetics can be selected to produce the next generation. More recent genetic techniques include **marker selected selection**, in which a genetic marker is used to screen for particular alleles associated with traits of interest. Such techniques have enabled farmers to improve the accuracy of their herd records and the certainty with which they select their breeding stock.

Selective Breeding and Genetic Gain in Cattle

Percentage genetic gain (y-axis, 0 to 80+) vs Years (x-axis, 0 to 40)

- Improvements due to marker assisted selection and transgenics
- Further gains using embryo transfer and sib-selection
- Gradual replacement of cows with EMT heifers from selected lines
- Gain due to more accurate assessment of genetic merit (breeding value)
- Testing of the first clone lines
- Steady progress using standard selection techniques and artificial insemination

Sources: Breeds of Livestock, Oklahoma State University and Genetics Australia.

Cattle are selected on the basis of particular desirable traits (e.g. milk solids or muscle mass). Most of the genetic improvement in dairy cattle has relied on selection of high quality progeny from proven stock and extensive use of superior sires through artificial insemination (AI). Improved breeding techniques accelerate the **genetic gain**, i.e. the gain toward the desirable phenotype of a breed. The graph (above) shows the predicted gains based on artificial insemination and standard selection techniques (based on criteria such as production or temperament). These are compared with the predicted gains using breeding values (the value of the genes to the progeny) and reproductive technologies such as embryo multiplication and transfer (EMT) of standard and transgenic stock, marker assisted selection, and sib-selection (selecting bulls on the basis of their sisters' performance).

The Perfect Dairy Cow

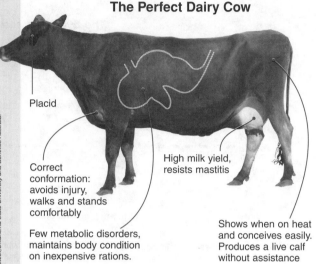

- Placid
- Correct conformation: avoids injury, walks and stands comfortably
- High milk yield, resists mastitis
- Few metabolic disorders, maintains body condition on inexpensive rations.
- Shows when on heat and conceives easily. Produces a live calf without assistance

Breeding programs select not only for milk production, but also for fertility, udder characteristics, and good health. In addition, artificial selection can be based on milk composition, e.g. high butterfat content (a feature of the Jersey breed, above).

A2 milk, which contains the A2 form of the beta casein protein, has recently received worldwide attention for claims that its consumption lowers the risk of childhood diabetes and coronary heart disease. Selection for the A2 variant in **Holstein cattle** has increased the proportion of A2 milk produced in some regions. A2 milk commands a higher price than A1 milk, so there is a commercial incentive to farmers to produce it.

1. Explain why artificial selection can effect changes in phenotype much more rapidly than can natural selection:

_____

_____

2. Suggest why selective breeding has proceeded particularly rapidly in dairy cattle: _____

_____

_____

3. Explain how molecular genetics has enhanced modern artificial selection techniques in the diary cow:

_____

_____

_____

The Evolution of Antibiotic Resistance

Antibiotic resistance arises when a genetic change allows bacteria to tolerate levels of antibiotic that would normally inhibit growth. This resistance may arise spontaneously, by induced mutation or copying error, or by transfer of genetic material between microbes. Genomic analyses from 30,000 year old permafrost sediments show that the genes for antibiotic resistance are not new. They have long been present in the bacterial genome, predating the modern selective pressure of antibiotic use. In the current selective environment, these genes have proliferated and antibiotic resistance has spread. For example, methicillin resistant strains of *Staphylococcus aureus* (MRSA) have acquired genes for resistance to all penicillins. Such strains are called superbugs.

The Evolution of Antibiotic Resistance in Bacteria

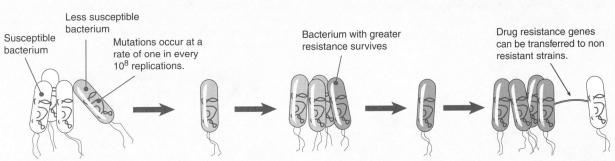

Susceptible bacterium

Less susceptible bacterium

Mutations occur at a rate of one in every 10^8 replications.

Bacterium with greater resistance survives

Drug resistance genes can be transferred to non resistant strains.

Any population, including bacterial populations, includes variants with unusual traits, in this case reduced sensitivity to an antibiotic. These variants arise as a result of mutations in the bacterial chromosome. Such mutations are well documented and some are ancient.

When a person takes an antibiotic, only the most susceptible bacteria will die. The more resistant cells remain and continue dividing. Note that the antibiotic does not create the resistance; it provides the environment in which selection for resistance can take place.

If the amount of antibiotic delivered is too low, or the course of antibiotics is not completed, a population of resistant bacteria develops. Within this population too, there will be variation in susceptibility. Some will survive higher antibiotic levels.

A highly resistant population has evolved. The resistant cells can exchange genetic material with other bacteria (via horizontal gene transmission), passing on the genes for resistance. The antibiotic initially used against this bacterial strain will now be ineffective.

Human Intervention in Evolution

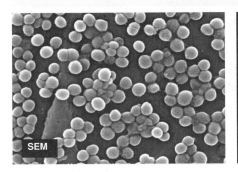

SEM

Staphylococcus aureus is a common bacterium responsible various minor skin infections in humans. MRSA (above) is variant strain that has evolved resistance to penicillin and related antibiotics. MRSA is troublesome in hospital-associated infections where patients with open wounds, invasive devices (e.g. catheters), and weakened immune systems are at greater risk for infection than the general public.

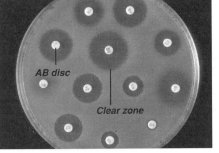

AB disc

Clear zone

The photo above shows an antibiogram plate culture of *Enterobacter sakazakii*, a rare cause of invasive infections in infants. An antibiogram measures the biological resistance of disease-causing organisms to antibiotic agents. The bacterial lawn (growth) on the agar plate is treated with antibiotic discs, and the sensitivity to various antibiotics is measured by the extent of the clearance zone in the bacterial lawn.

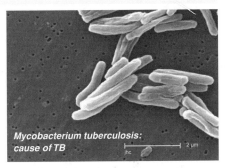

Mycobacterium tuberculosis: cause of TB

2 μm

TB is a disease that has experienced spectacular ups and downs. Drugs were developed to treat it, but then people became complacent when they thought the disease was beaten. TB has since resurged because patients stop their medication too soon and infect others. Today, one in seven new TB cases is resistant to the two drugs most commonly used as treatments, and 5% of these patients die.

1. Describe two ways in which antibiotic resistance can become widespread:

    (a) _____

    (b) _____

2. Genomic evidence indicates that the genes for antibiotic resistance are ancient:

    (a) How could these genes have arisen in the first place? _____

    _____

    (b) Why were they not lost from the bacterial genome? _____

    _____

    (c) Explain why these genes are proliferating now: _____

    _____

    _____

© BIOZONE International 2006-2011
ISBN: 978-1-877462-98-6
Photocopying Prohibited

Periodicals: The enemy within

Related activities: Resistance in Pathogens

Chloroquine Resistance in Protozoa

Chloroquine is an antimalarial drug, discovered in 1934, and first used clinically to prevent malaria in 1946. Chloroquine was widely used because it was cheap to produce, safe, and very effective. Chloroquine resistance in *Plasmodium falciparum* first appeared in the late 1950s, and the subsequent spread of resistance has significantly decreased chloroquine's effectiveness. The WHO regularly update the global status on anti-malarial drug efficacy and drug resistance. Their 2010 report shows that when chloroquine is used as a monotherapy, it is still effective at preventing malaria in Central American countries (chloroquine resistance has not yet developed there). In 30 other countries, chloroquine failure rates ranged between 20-100%. In some regions, chloroquine used in combination with other anti-malarial drugs is still an effective treatment.

Global Spread of Chloroquine Resistance

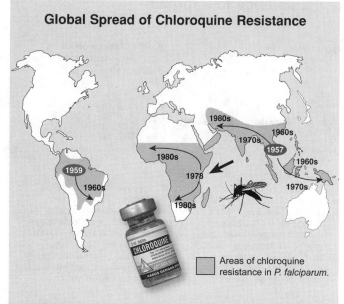

Areas of chloroquine resistance in *P. falciparum*.

Malaria in humans is caused by various species of *Plasmodium*, a protozoan parasite transmitted by *Anopheles* mosquitoes. The inexpensive antimalarial drug **chloroquine** was used successfully to treat malaria for many years, but its effectiveness has declined since resistance to the drug was first recorded in the 1950s. Chloroquine resistance has spread steadily (above) and now two of the four *Plasmodium* species, *P. falciparum* and *P. vivax* are chloroquine-resistant. *P. falciparum* alone accounts for 80% of all human malarial infections and 90% of the deaths, so this rise in resistance is of global concern. New anti-malarial drugs have been developed, but are expensive and often have undesirable side effects. Resistance to even these newer drugs is already evident, especially in *P. falciparum*, although this species is currently still susceptible to artemisinin, a derivative of the medicinal herb *Artemisia annua*.

Recent studies have demonstrated a link between mutations in the chloroquine resistance transporter (PfCRT) gene, and resistance to chloroquine in *P. falciparum*. PfCRT is a membrane protein involved in drug and metabolite transport.

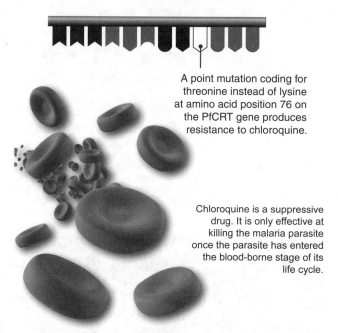

A point mutation coding for threonine instead of lysine at amino acid position 76 on the PfCRT gene produces resistance to chloroquine.

Chloroquine is a suppressive drug. It is only effective at killing the malaria parasite once the parasite has entered the blood-borne stage of its life cycle.

The use of chloroquine in many African countries was halted during the 1990s because resistance developed in *P. falciparum*. Recent studies in Malawi and Kenya have revealed a significant decrease in chloroquine resistance since the drug was withdrawn. There may be a significant fitness cost to the PfCRT mutants in the absence of anti-malaria drugs, leading to their decline in frequency once the selection pressure of the drugs is removed. This raises the possibility of re-introducing chloroquine as an anti-malarial treatment in the future.

1. Describe the benefits of using chloroquine to prevent malaria: _____

_____

_____

2. With reference to *Plasmodium falciparum*, explain how chloroquine resistance arises: _____

_____

_____

_____

3. Describe two strategies to reduce the spread of chloroquine resistance while still treating malaria:

(a) _____

_____

(b) _____

_____

Related activities: Malaria, Drug Resistance in HIV

Periodicals: Beating the bloodsuckers

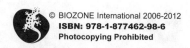

© BIOZONE International 2006-2012
ISBN: 978-1-877462-98-6
Photocopying Prohibited

Antigenic Variability in Viruses

Influenza (flu) is a disease of the upper respiratory tract caused by strains of the *Influenzavirus*. Globally, up to 500,000 people die from influenza every year. It is estimated that up to 20% of Britons are affected by the flu annually, and a small number of deaths occur as a result. Three types of *Influenzavirus* affect humans. They are simply named *Influenzavirus* A, B, and C. The most common and most virulent of these strains is *Influenzavirus* A, which is discussed in more detail below. Influenza viruses are constantly undergoing genetic changes. **Antigenic drifts** are small changes in the virus which happen continually over time. Such changes mean that the influenza vaccine must be adjusted each year to include the most recently circulating influenza viruses. **Antigenic shift** occurs when two or more different viral strains (or different viruses) combine to form a new subtype. The changes are large and sudden and most people lack immunity to the new subtype. New influenza viruses arising from antigenic shift have caused influenza pandemics that have killed millions of people over the last century.

Structure of *Influenzavirus*

Viral strains are identified by the variation in their H and N surface antigens. Viruses are able to combine and readily rearrange their RNA segments, which alters the protein composition of their H and N glycoprotein spikes.

The *influenzavirus* is surrounded by an **envelope** containing protein and lipids.

The genetic material is actually closely surrounded by protein capsomeres (these have been omitted here and below right in order to illustrate the changes in the RNA more clearly).

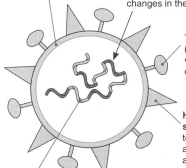

The **neuraminidase (N) spikes** help the virus to detach from the cell after infection.

Hemagglutinin (H) spikes allow the virus to recognize and attach to cells before attacking them.

The viral genome is contained on **eight RNA segments**, which enables the exchange of genes between different viral strains.

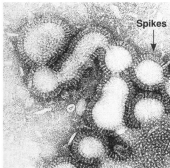

Spikes

Photo right: *Electron micrograph of Influenzavirus showing the glycoprotein spikes projecting from the viral envelope*

Antigenic Shift in *Influenzavirus*

Influenza vaccination is the primary method for preventing influenza and is 75% effective. The ability of the virus to recombine its RNA enables it to change each year, so that different strains dominate in any one season. The 'flu' vaccination is updated annually to incorporate the antigenic properties of currently circulating strains. Three strains are chosen for each year's vaccination. Selection is based on estimates of which strains will be predominant in the following year.

H1N1, H1N2, and H3N2 (below) are the known *Influenza A* viral subtypes currently circulating among humans. Although the body will have acquired antibodies from previous flu strains, the new combination of N and H spikes is sufficiently different to enable new viral strains to avoid detection by the immune system. The World Health Organisation coordinates strain selection for each year's influenza vaccine.

H1N1   H1N2   H3N2

Human Intervention in Evolution

1. The *Influenzavirus* is able to mutate readily and alter the composition of H and N spikes on its surface.

   (a) Explain why this is the case: _____

   _____

   _____

   (b) Explain how this affects the ability of the immune system to recognize the virus and launch an attack:

   _____

   _____

   _____

2. Discuss why a virus capable of antigenic shift is more dangerous to humans than a virus undergoing antigenic drift:

   _____

   _____

   _____

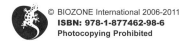 © BIOZONE International 2006-2011
ISBN: 978-1-877462-98-6
Photocopying Prohibited

Periodicals: Tracking the next killer flu

Related activities: The Influenza Threat
Weblinks: Antigenic Shift in Influenza

A 2

Drug Resistance in HIV

Although many diseases are treated very effectively with drugs, the emergence of drug resistant pathogens is increasingly undermining the ability to treat and control diseases such as HIV/AIDS. HIV's high mutation rate and short generation times contribute to the rapid spread of drug resistance. Rapid evolution in pathogens is exacerbated by the strong selection pressures created by the wide use and misuse of antiviral drugs, the poor quality of available drugs in some sectors of the population, and lack of education on drug use. The most successful treatment for several diseases, including HIV/AIDS, appears to be a multi-pronged attack using a cocktail of drugs to target the pathogen in several different ways.

Drug Resistance in HIV

Strains of drug-resistant HIV arise when the virus mutates during replication. Resistance may develop as a result of a single mutation, or through a step-wise accumulation of specific mutations. These mutations may alter drug binding capacity or increase viral fitness, or they may be naturally occurring polymorphisms (which occur in untreated patients). Drug resistance is likely to develop in patients who do not follow their treatment schedule closely, as the virus has an opportunity to adapt more readily to a "non-lethal" drug dose. The best practice for managing the HIV virus is to treat it with a cocktail of anti-retroviral drugs with different actions to minimize the number of viruses in the body. This minimizes the replication rate, and also the chance of a drug resistant mutation being produced.

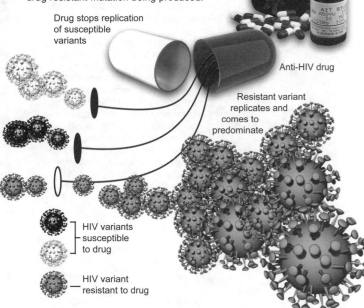

Drug stops replication of susceptible variants

Anti-HIV drug

Resistant variant replicates and comes to predominate

HIV variants susceptible to drug

HIV variant resistant to drug

Causes of Drug Resistance

- Poor drug compliance: patients stop taking their medication or do not follow the treatment as directed.

- Low levels of drug absorption: drug absorption is reduced if a patient has diarrhoea, is vomiting, or has an intestinal infection.

- Individual variation: the effectiveness of the body to absorb, distribute, metabolise, and eliminate a drug varies between patients.

- Toxicity: the side effects of the medication may make the patient very sick, so they stop taking it.

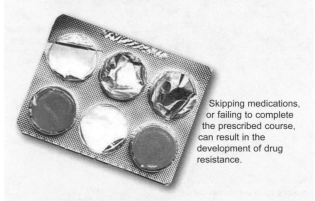

Skipping medications, or failing to complete the prescribed course, can result in the development of drug resistance.

Superinfection arises when a person already infected with HIV acquires a second strain of the virus. Superinfection increases the body's viral load, and can speed up disease progression or result in the patient acquiring a drug resistant HIV strain. The phenomenon of superinfection has implications for the development of a successful HIV vaccine because it shows that the body does not develop an immunological memory to HIV. This means that future HIV vaccines may be ineffective at preventing HIV infection.

1. Describe factors contributing to the rapid spread of drug resistance in pathogens: _____

_____

_____

2. With reference to HIV/AIDS, explain how drug resistance arises in a pathogen population: _____

_____

_____

_____

_____

3. Explain the implications of HIV superinfection on the development of a successful HIV vaccine: _____

_____

_____

_____

Related activities: *Chloroquine Resistance in Protozoa*

Periodicals:
Search for a cure

© BIOZONE International 2006-2012
ISBN: 978-1-877462-98-6
Photocopying Prohibited

Insecticide Resistance

Insecticides are pesticides used to control insects considered harmful to humans, their livelihood, or environment. Insecticides have been used for hundreds of years, but their use has proliferated since the advent of synthetic insecticides (e.g. DDT) in the 1940s. When **insecticide resistance** develops the control agent will no longer control the target species. Insecticide resistance can arise through a combination of behavioral, anatomical, biochemical, and physiological mechanisms, but the underlying process is a form of **natural selection**, in which the most resistant organisms survive to pass on their genes to their offspring. To combat increasing resistance, higher doses of more potent pesticides are sometimes used. This drives the selection process, so that increasingly higher dose rates are required to combat rising resistance. This cycle is made worse by the development of multiple resistance in some pest species. High application rates may also kill non-target species, and persistent chemicals may remain in the environment and accumulate in food chains. These concerns have led to some insecticides being banned (DDT has been banned in most developed countries since the 1970s). Insecticides are used in medical, agricultural, and environmental applications, so the development of resistance has serious environmental and economic consequences.

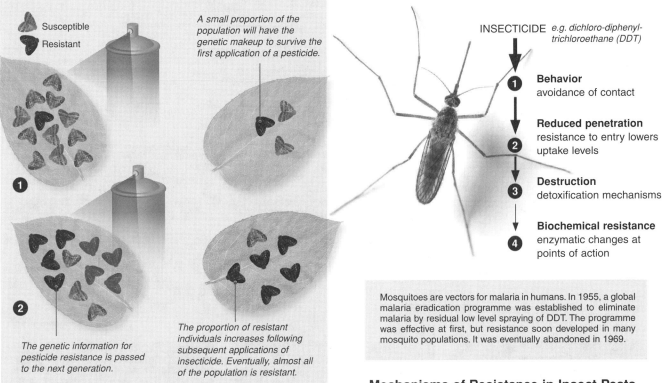

Susceptible

Resistant

A small proportion of the population will have the genetic makeup to survive the first application of a pesticide.

INSECTICIDE *e.g. dichloro-diphenyl-trichloroethane (DDT)*

1 **Behavior** avoidance of contact

2 **Reduced penetration** resistance to entry lowers uptake levels

3 **Destruction** detoxification mechanisms

4 **Biochemical resistance** enzymatic changes at points of action

The genetic information for pesticide resistance is passed to the next generation.

The proportion of resistant individuals increases following subsequent applications of insecticide. Eventually, almost all of the population is resistant.

Mosquitoes are vectors for malaria in humans. In 1955, a global malaria eradication programme was established to eliminate malaria by residual low level spraying of DDT. The programme was effective at first, but resistance soon developed in many mosquito populations. It was eventually abandoned in 1969.

Human Intervention in Evolution

The Development of Resistance

The application of an insecticide can act as a potent selection pressure for resistance in pest insects. The insecticide acts as a selective agent, and only individuals with greater natural resistance survive the application to pass on their genes to the next generation. These genes (or combination of genes) may spread through all subsequent populations.

Mechanisms of Resistance in Insect Pests

Insecticide resistance in insects can arise through a combination of mechanisms. (1) Increased sensitivity to an insecticide will cause the pest to avoid a treated area. (2) Certain genes (e.g. the *PEN* gene) confer stronger physical barriers, decreasing the rate at which the chemical penetrates the cuticle. (3) Detoxification by enzymes within the insect's body can render the pesticide harmless, and (4) structural changes to the target enzymes make the pesticide ineffective. No single mechanism provides total immunity, but together they transform the effect from potentially lethal to insignificant.

1. Give two reasons why widespread insecticide resistance can develop very rapidly in insect populations:

   (a) _____

   (b) _____

2. Explain how repeated insecticide applications act as a selective agent for evolutionary change in insect populations:

   _____

   _____

3. With reference to synthetic insecticides, discuss the implications of insecticide resistance to human populations:

   _____

   _____

   _____

© BIOZONE International 2006-2011
ISBN: 978-1-877462-98-6
Photocopying Prohibited

Related activities: Drug Resistance in HIV, Antibiotic Resistance,
Chloroquine Resistance in Protozoa

RA 2

Global Warming and Population Change

Since the last significant period of climate change at the end of the ice age 10,000 years ago, plants and animals have adapted to survive in their current habitats. Accelerated global warming is again changing the habitats that plants and animals live in and this could have significant effects on the biodiversity of specific regions as well as on the planet overall. As temperatures rise, organisms will be forced to move to new areas where temperatures are similar to their current level. Those that cannot move face extinction, as temperatures move outside their limits of tolerance. Changes in precipitation as a result of climate change also affect where organisms can live. Long term changes in climate could see the contraction of many organisms' habitats while at the same time the expansion of others. Habitat migration (the shift of a habitat from its current region to another), will also occur more often. Already there are a number of cases showing the effects of climate change on a range of organisms.

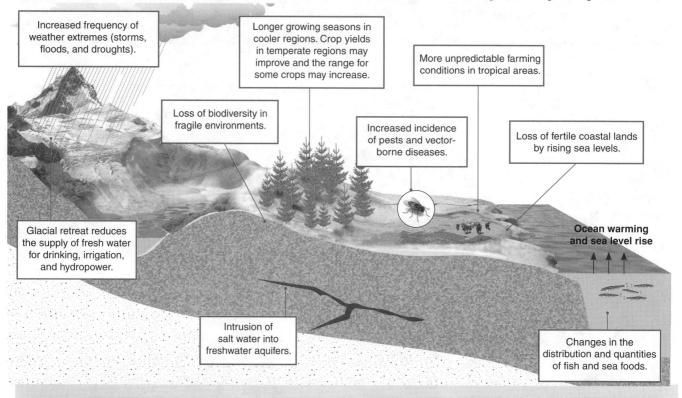

Increased frequency of weather extremes (storms, floods, and droughts).

Longer growing seasons in cooler regions. Crop yields in temperate regions may improve and the range for some crops may increase.

More unpredictable farming conditions in tropical areas.

Loss of biodiversity in fragile environments.

Increased incidence of pests and vector-borne diseases.

Loss of fertile coastal lands by rising sea levels.

Glacial retreat reduces the supply of fresh water for drinking, irrigation, and hydropower.

Ocean warming and sea level rise

Intrusion of salt water into freshwater aquifers.

Changes in the distribution and quantities of fish and sea foods.

Studies of forests in the United States have shown that although there will be increases and decreases in the distribution ranges of various tree species, overall there will be an 11% decrease in forest cover, with an increase in savanna and arid woodland. Communities of oak/pine and oak/hickory are predicted to increase in range while spruce/fir and maple/beech/birch communities will decrease.

Photo: Walter Siegmund

Studies of the distributions of butterfly species in many countries show their populations are shifting. Surveys of Edith's checkerspot butterfly (*Euphydryas editha*) in western North America have shown it to be moving north and to higher altitudes.

An Australian study in 2004 found the center of distribution for the AdhS gene in *Drosophila*, which helps survival in hot and dry conditions, had shifted 400 kilometres south in the last twenty years.

Studies of sea life along the Californian coast have shown that between 1931 and 1996, shoreline ocean temperatures increased by 0.79°C and populations of invertebrates including sea stars, limpets and snails moved northward in their distributions.

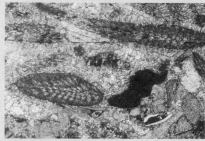

A 2009 study of 200 million year old plant fossils from Greenland has provided evidence of a sudden collapse in biodiversity that is correlated with, and appears to be caused by, a very slight rise in CO_2 levels.

Weblinks: *Climate Change*

Periodicals:
Unnatural selection,
In the blink of an eye

© BIOZONE International 2006-2012
ISBN: 978-1-877462-98-6
Photocopying Prohibited

Effects of increases in temperature on animal populations

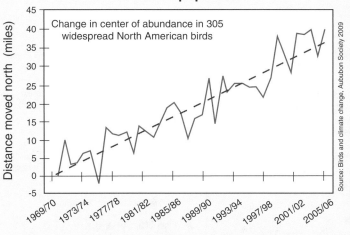

Change in center of abundance in 305 widespread North American birds

Distance moved north (miles)

Source: Birds and climate change. Aububon Society 2009

Animals living at altitude are also affected by warming climates and are being forced to shift their normal range. As temperatures increase, the snow line increases in altitude pushing alpine animals to higher altitudes. In some areas of North America this has resulting the local extinction of the North American pika (*Ochotona princeps*).

Wiki Commons

A number of studies indicate that animals are beginning to be affected by increases in global temperatures. Data sets from around the world show that birds are migrating up to two weeks earlier to summer feeding grounds and are often not migrating as far in winter.

1. Describe some of the likely effects of global warming on physical aspects of the environment: _____

_____

_____

_____

2. (a) Using the information on this and the previous activity, discuss the probable effects of global warming on plant crops:

_____

_____

(b) Suggest how farmers might be able to adjust to these changes: _____

_____

_____

_____

3. Discuss the evidence that insect populations are affected by global temperature: _____

_____

_____

4. (a) Describe how increases in global temperatures have affected some migratory birds: _____

_____

_____

(b) Explain how these changes in migratory patterns might affect food availability for these populations: _____

_____

_____

5. Explain how global warming could lead to the local extinction of some alpine species: _____

_____

_____

_____

Periodicals:
Enter the Anthropocene
- age of man

Appendix

THE ORIGIN AND EVOLUTION OF LIFE

▶ **Life's Far Flung Raw Materials**
Scientific American, July 1999, pp. 26-33. *Experimental evidence supports the idea that the complex organic molecules of life may have arisen within interstellar clouds.*

▶ **The Ice of Life**
Scientific American, August 2001, pp. 37-41. *Space ice may promote organic molecules and may have seeded life on Earth (teacher's reference).*

▶ **A Simpler Origin of Life**
Scientific American, June 2007, pp. 24-31. *Two theories on the origin of RNA (teacher's reference).*

▶ **Primeval Pools**
New Scientist, 2 July 2005, pp. 40-43. *Ecosystems where microbes dominate as they did millions of years in the past.*

▶ **Earth in the Beginning**
National Geographic, 210(6) Dec. 2006, pp. 58-67. *Modern landscapes offer glimpses of the way Earth may have looked billions of years ago.*

▶ **The Rise of Life on Earth**
National Geographic, 193(3) March 1998, pp. 54-81. *A series of articles covering the theories for life's origins, the evolution of life's diversity, and the origin of eukaryotic cells.*

▶ **A Cool Early Life**
Scientific American, Oct. 2005, pp. 40-47. *Evidence suggests that the Earth cooled as early as 4.4 bya. These cooler, wet surroundings were necessary for life to evolve.*

THE EVIDENCE FOR EVOLUTION

▶ **Meet your Ancestor**
New Scientist, 9 Sept. 2006, pp. 35-39. *The significance of a recent fossil find: the link between fish and tetrapods.*

▶ **The Quick and the Dead**
New Scientist, 5 June 1999, pp. 44-48. *The formation of fossils: fossil types and preservation in different environments.*

▶ **How Old is...**
National Geographic, 200(3) Sept. 2001, pp. 79-101. *A discussion of dating methods and their application.*

▶ **The Accidental Discovery of a Feathered Giant Dinosaur**
Biol. Sci. Rev., 20(4), April 2008, pp. 18-20. *How scientists piece together and interpret confusing fossil evidence.*

▶ **Uprooting the Tree of Life**
Scientific American Feb. 2000, pp. 72-77. *Using molecular techniques to redefine phylogeny and divulge the path of evolution.*

▶ **Regulating Evolution**
Sci. American, May 2008, pp. 34-45. *Mutations in the DNA switches controlling body-shaping genes, rather than the genes themselves, have been significant in the evolution of morphological differences.*

▶ **A Fin is a Limb is a Wing- How Evolution Fashioned its Masterworks**
National Geographic, 210(5) Nov. 2006, pp. 110-135. *An excellent account of the role of developmental genes in the evolution of complex organs and structures in animals. Beautifully illustrated, compelling evidence for the mechanisms of evolutionary change.*

▶ **A Waste of Space**
New Scientist, 25 April 1998, pp. 38-39. *Vestigial organs: how they arise in an evolutionary sense and the role they might play.*

MECHANISMS OF EVOLUTION

▶ **Was Darwin Wrong?**
National Geographic, 206(5) Nov. 2004, pp. 2-35. *The evidence for evolution. A good way to remind students that the scientific debate around evolutionary theory is associated with the mechanisms by which evolution occurs, not the fact of evolution itself.*

▶ **Skin Deep**
Scientific American, October 2002, pp. 50-57. *This article examines the evolution of skin colour in humans and presents powerful evidence for skin colour ("race") being the end result of opposing selection forces (the need for protection of folate from UV vs the need to absorb vitamin D). Clearly written and of high interest, this is a must for student discussion and a perfect vehicle for examining natural selection.*

▶ **Fair Enough**
New Scientist, 12 Oct. 2002, pp. 34-37. *Skin colour in humans: this article examines the argument for there being a selective benefit to being dark or pale in different environments.*

▶ **The Moths of War**
New Scientist, 8 Dec. 2007, pp 46-49. *New research into the melanism of the peppered moth reaffirms it as an example of evolution, reclaiming it back from Creationists.*

▶ **Polymorphism**
Biol. Sci. Rev., 14(1) Sept. 2001, pp. 19-21. *A good account of genetic polymorphism. Examples include the carbonaria gene (Biston), the sickle cell gene, and aphids.*

▶ **Genetics of Sickle Cell Anaemia**
Biol. Sci. Rev., 20(4) April 2008, pp. 14-17. *This account includes*

explanation of how a mutation is retained in the population as a result of heterozygous advantage.

▶ **Black Squirrels**
Biol. Sci. Rev., 21(2), Nov. 2008, pp. 39-41. *A look at how squirrel types have changed in Britain over time, and the selection pressures acting on the pigmentation and melanism.*

▶ **The Hardy-Weinberg Principle**
Biol. Sci. Rev., 15(4), April 2003, pp. 7-9. *A succinct explanation of the basis of the Hardy-Weinberg principle, and its uses in estimating genotype frequencies and predicting change in populations.*

▶ **The Cheetah: Losing the Race?**
Biol. Sci. Rev., 14(2) Nov. 2001, pp. 7-10. *The inbred status of cheetahs and its evolutionary consequences.*

▶ **Animal Attraction**
National Geographic, July 2003, pp. 28-55. *An engaging and expansive account of mating in the animal world.*

▶ **Species and Species Formation**
Biol. Sci. Rev., 20(3), Feb. 2008, pp. 36-39. *A feature covering the definition of species and how new species come into being through speciation.*

▶ **What is a Species?**
Scientific American June 2008, pp. 48-55. *The science of classification; modern and traditional approaches, and the importance of taxonomy to identifying and recognising diversity.*

▶ **Cichlids of the Rift Lakes**
Biol. Sci. Rev., 14(2) Nov. 2001, pp. 7-10. *The inbred status of cheetahs and its evolutionary consequences.*

▶ **Listen, We're Different**
New Scientist, 17 July 1999, pp. 32-35. *An account of speciation in periodic cicadas as a result of behavioural and temporal isolating mechanisms.*

▶ **Evolution in New Zealand**
Biol. Sci. Rev., 21(3) Feb. 2009, pp. 33-37. *NZ offers a unique suite of case studies in evolution*

PATTERNS OF EVOLUTION

▶ **Dinosaurs take Wing**
National Geographic, 194(1) July 1998, pp. 74-99. *An account of the evolution of birds from small theropod dinosaurs, including an exploration of the homology between the typical dinosaur limb and the wing of the modern bird. An excellent account.*

▶ **Evolution: Five Big Questions**
New Scientist, 14 June 2003, pp. 32-39, 48-51. *A synopsis of the five most common points of discussion regarding evolution and the mechanisms by which it occurs.*

Appendix

▶ **Evolution in the Fast Lane**

New Scientist, 2 April 2011, pp. 32-36. *The evolution of stickleback armour provides an example of rapid evolution. Fluctuating selection pressures produce unexpected patterns of evolution in algal and rotifer populations also. It seems that rapid evolution may not be the exception, but the norm.*

▶ **Which Came First?**

Scientific American, Feb. 1997, pp. 12-14. *Shared features among fossils; convergence or common ancestry?*

▶ **The Rise of Mammals**

National Geographic, 203(4), pp. April 2003, p. 2-37. *An account of the adaptive radiation of mammals and the significance of the placenta in mammalian evolution.*

▶ **Evolution in New Zealand**

Biol. Sci. Rev., 21(3) Feb. 2009, pp. 33-37. *NZ offers a unique suite of case studies in evolution*

▶ **Mass Extinctions**

New Scientist, 5 March 2011, pp i-iv. *An 'instant expert' article covering the nature of mass extinction using two important mass extinction events as examples: the loss of the dinosaurs and the end Permian extinction which resulted in the loss of 80-90% of species. It also describes how life rebounds following extinction events.*

▶ **The Sixth Extinction**

National Geographic, 195(2) Feb. 1999, pp. 42-59. *High extinction rates have occurred five times in the past. Human impact is driving the sixth extinction.*

HUMAN INTERVENTION IN EVOLUTION

▶ **Taming the Wild**

National Geographic, 219(3) March 2011, pp. 34-59. *Species that have been successfully domesticated and live with human contact have different genetic traits to those that are not domesticated. An experiment in fox breeding begun in the 1960s showed after nine generations a collection of genes conferring tame behavior.*

▶ **The Enemy Within**

Scientific American, April 2011, pp. 26-33. *Antibiotic resistance is spreading in the transfer of genes that confer resistance in a new pattern globally. New medications are not being developed quickly enough to treat gram-negative bacteria.*

▶ **Beating the Bloodsuckers**

Biol. Sci. Rev., 16(3) Feb. 2004, pp. 31-35. *The global distribution of malaria, the current state of malaria research, and an account of the biology of the Plasmodium parasite and the body's immune response to it.*

▶ **Tracking the Next Killer Flu**

National Geographic, 208(4) Oct. 2005, pp. 4-31. *Discussion on flu viruses and how they spread.*

▶ **Search for a Cure**

National Geographic, 201(2) February 2002, pp. 32-43. *An account of the status of the AIDS epidemic and the measures to stop it.*

▶ **Unnatural Selection**

New Scientist, 30 April 2011, pp. 32-37. *The impact of humans on evolution through selective hunting, global warming, poisoning and the spread of antibiotic resistance, introduction of alien species, and spread of disease. A thought provoking account.*

▶ **In the Blink of an Eye**

New Scientist, 9 July 2005, pp. 28-31. *Rapid contemporary evolution may be widespread and humans may be unwittingly helping it along.*

▶ **Enter the Anthropocene - Age of Man**

National Geographic, 219(3) March 2011, pp. 60-85. *The current and likely future impact of humans on the Earth's biological and geological systems.*

LATIN & GREEK ROOTS, PREFIXES, & SUFFIXES

Many biological terms have a Latin origin. Understanding the meaning of the Latin component of a word will help you to understand and remember its meaning and predict the probable meaning of new words. A small collection of roots is provided below, together with an illustrative example.

a(n)- without................................ anoxic
amphi- both...........................amphibian
ante- before ....antenatal
anthro- human...................anthropology
anti- against, opposite............ antibiotic
aqua- water...............................aquatic
arach- spider ....arachnoid
arbor- tree ....arboreal
arch(ae/i)- ancient.................... Archaea
arthro- joint...........................arthropod
artio- even-numbered .... artiodactyl
avi- bird.. avian
axi- axis.....................................axillary
branch- gill..............................branchial
cauda- tail..................................caudal
centi- hundred ....centimeter
ceph(al)- head ....cephalothorax
cera(s)(t)- horn.....................ceratopsian
dactyl- finger......................polydactylic
deci-(a) ten .... decibel, decapod
dendr- tree ....dendrogram
dent- tooth...............................edentate
derm- skin...........................pachyderm
di- two ....dihybrid

dors- back...................................dorsal
ecto- outside..........................ectoderm
endo- inside.......................endoparasite
equi- horse, equal................ equilibrium
erect- upright .... Homo erectus
eu- well, very.........................eukaryote
exo- outside ....exoskeleton
foramen- opening ..... foramen magnum
gast(e)r- stomach, pouch ..... gastropod
gymn- naked.....................gymnosperm
hal- salty ....halophyte
haplo- single, simple.................haploid
holo- complete, whole.............. holozoic
hydr- water.............................hydrophyte
hyper- above.........................hypertonic
hypo- beneath.......................hypotonic
inter- between ....interspecific
intra- within............................intraspecific
iso- equal .... isotonic
kilo- thousand ....kilogram
leuc- white.............................leucocyte
lip- fat......................................lipoprotein
lith- stone ....Palaeolithic
lumen- cavity..............................lumen
mamma- breast.......................mammal
mega- large.........................megafauna
melan- black ....melanocyte
meso- middle.........................Mesolithic
meta- after.....................metamorphosis
mono- one...........................monohybrid
morph- form ....morphology
neo- new ....Neolithic
notho- southern...................Nothofagus
os(s/t)- bone...........................osteocyte
palae- old...........................Palaeocene
pect(or)- chest....................pectoral fin
ped- foot ....quadraped
pent- five....................pentadactyl limb
pod- foot ....sauropod
pre- before ....premolar
pro- in front of ....Prokaryote
prot- first..................................protobiont
pseud- false....................... pseudopodia
pter- wing, fern......................Pterophyta
rhin- nose, snout ....rhinoceros
seba- tallow, wax .... sebaceous
semi- half ....semi-conservative
soma- body...............................somatic
sperm- seed..................spermatophyte
sphinct- closing ....sphincter
stom- mouth................................stoma
strat- layer......................... stratification
sub- below ....subtidal
super- beyond........................superior
supra- above...........supracoracoideus
un- one .... unicellular
uro- tail ....urodele
vas- vessel............................. vascular
ventr- belly .... ventral
vitr- glass ....in vitro
xen- stranger ....xenotransplant
xer- dry ....xerophyte
xyl- wood.....................................xylem
zo- animal ....zoological

Index

© BIOZONE International 2006-2012